D1329868

# OBJECTS OF THOUGHT

A. N. PRIOR

# OBJECTS OF
# THOUGHT

*Edited by P. T. Geach*
*and A. J. P. Kenny*

OXFORD
AT THE CLARENDON PRESS
1971

*Oxford University Press, Ely House, London W.1*

GLASGOW  NEW YORK  TORONTO  MELBOURNE  WELLINGTON
CAPE TOWN  SALISBURY  IBADAN  NAIROBI  DAR ES SALAAM  LUSAKA  ADDIS ABABA
BOMBAY  CALCUTTA  MADRAS  KARACHI  LAHORE  DACCA
KUALA LUMPUR  SINGAPORE  HONG KONG  TOKYO

PRINTED IN GREAT BRITAIN

# CONTENTS

# EDITORIAL NOTE

THE oldest part of this book can be traced back to a 100-page typescript circulated by Arthur Prior to a few friends and colleagues in 1964, which contained five chapters entitled 'Propositions and Facts', 'Propositions and Sentences', 'Platonism and Quantification', 'Extensionality and Propositional Identity', 'A Budget of Paradoxes'.

At his death Prior left the manuscript of a work entitled 'Objects of Thought'. In the same file he left two sets of notes giving the plan of the work. The first is dated 18 April 1965 and reads as follows:

> This course begins to acquire a structure: I. What we think. I. 1. What we think and what we think about. I. 2. Propositions (and facts) are logical constructions. I. 3. The Logic of belief (a) Paradoxes. I. 4. The Logic of belief: Believing and saying (Moore's paradox). I. 5. Specific laws of belief? II. 1. The 4 possibilities. II. 2–5. Each in turn.

The second is undated, but is clearly considerably later. It reads:

Ch. 1. Props. and Facts.

Ch. 2. Props. and Sentences.

Ch. 3. Platonism and Quantification (add bit about Cohen's leading to interesting formal developments).

Ch. 4. Extensionality etc. Insert stuff about 'definition' of truth-functions $Np = Dpp$. Yet perhaps $KBxNpNBxDpp$.

Ch. 5. Imperatives and Interrogatives.

Ch. 6. A Budget of Paradoxes. Add bit at end about Cohen's treatment.

(insertion in margin) Tarski etc.

Ch. 8.[1] Relations and Intentionality. Reid, Findlay, (Quine), Anscombe.

Ch. 9. The obvious solution. Reid etc. often have *general* objects. Quantifiers inside and outside intentional operators. Singular cases (Quine). Concealed quantification solution. Removal of need to talk about referential opacity. Application to the Castañeda sophisma. Difficulties. (At this point?)

---

[1] The '8' here is corrected from '7', and '9' from '8' below.

Ch. 10. Russellian names and descriptions. Mill. Russell. Difficulties.

Ch. 11. Alternative logical grammars (empty names). Objections
to 'intention' theory (of Kenny). But perhaps no names—
consequences.

From the first of these two sketches we took the division of the
work into two parts, and the titles which were clearly intended
for them.

Of the eleven chapters listed in the second sketch, we found
ten among the manuscripts. They were in varying states of
completeness.

Ch. 1 was complete and prepared for the press.

Ch. 2 was complete and prepared for the press.

Ch. 3 was complete and prepared for the press except for
section 6 which existed only in a possibly unfinished manuscript.

Ch. 4 was complete and prepared for the press except for gaps
in footnotes, which we completed within square brackets.

Ch. 5 was complete and prepared for the press except for gaps
in footnotes.

Ch. 6 contained manuscript insertions in sections 1–4 consisting of proofs which at a certain stage Prior had intended to
relegate to an appendix. Sections 5 and 6 were wholly in manuscript but presented no textual problems.

(Chapters 1, 2, 3, 4, and 6 are amplified versions of the five
chapters of the 1964 version. Ch. 5 on internal evidence was
written in autumn 1965 when Prior was in Los Angeles.)

Ch. 7, as can be seen from the draft list of contents, was an
afterthought. It was entirely in manuscript and we had occa-
sionally to choose between doublets: for details see the note
on p. 107.

Ch. 8 was entirely in manuscript. A certain amount of surgery
was necessary: for details see notes on pp. 112, 128.

Ch. 9 was entirely in manuscript: no alterations were needed
except for the excision of one doublet.

Ch. 10 consisted of an incomplete manuscript, with a note
indicating that a passage from Prior's paper 'Is the Concept of
Referential Opacity Really Necessary?' was to be inserted. We
have inserted the appropriate passage with slight adaptation to
make it fit the context. Some rearrangement of paragraphs was
needed on the last page of this chapter.

Ch. 11 was not to be found in the file. As the draft list of contents indicated that in this chapter Prior intended to discuss systems with empty names and to criticize Kenny's 'intention' theory, we have included in an appendix a hitherto unpublished paper on 'Names', written some time between 1963 and 1966, in which these topics are treated. It has been placed in an appendix to indicate that it was not filed by Prior himself with the materials for this book.

What is presented in the body of the book consists entirely of Prior's own words intended by him for inclusion in *Objects of Thought*. Editorial work has been restricted to slight rearrangement and occasional excision, plus the provision of footnote references in square brackets. We have therefore left the work in an incomplete and unpolished form. Naturally, Prior himself would not have published it without substantial revisions and additions, and at times he seemed in two minds about completing it in exact accordance with his original plan. He did not lose interest in the problems it concerns, nor did he grow dissatisfied with his solutions to them, but had he lived he might have wished to set them within the context of his more recent researches.

We wish to thank the Editor of *Critica* for permission to reprint Ch. 6 which first appeared in that periodical, the Editor of *Acta Philosophica Fennica* for permission to reproduce some material in Ch. 10, and the North-Holland Publishing Company for permission to incorporate in the Appendix most of a paper which appeared in *Formal Systems and Recursive Functions*.

We are greatly indebted to Mrs. Mary Prior, who discovered the manuscripts printed in this volume, who invited us to edit them for publication, and who assisted us in many ways in preparing the volume for the press, especially by compiling the Index.

PETER THOMAS GEACH

ANTHONY KENNY

# PART I

# WHAT WE THINK

# 1

## PROPOSITIONS AND FACTS

1. *The senses of 'object of thought'.* The phrase 'object of thought' may be used in two very different ways. An object of thought may be (1) what we think, or (2) what we think *about*; e.g. if we think that grass is green, (1) what we think is *that grass is green*, and (2) what we think about is *grass*. 'Objects of thought' in the first sense are Ryle's 'accusatives of belief';[1] they are sometimes called 'propositions', not in the sense of sentences, but in the sense of what sentences mean. Objects of thought in this first sense will be the topic of Part I, but note first that this is not a very usual or natural sense of the phrase. By an object of thought we usually mean something that we are thinking *about*, i.e. an 'object of thought' in sense (2); though this is also often called the 'subject' of our thought, and it is usually the grammatical subject of the sentence (if any) by which our thought is expressed. The distinction between what we think and what we think about is of course paralleled in speech by that between what we say (e.g. again, that grass is green), and what we are speaking about (e.g. grass).

Note also that, given that we think about some object (or subject), there is yet a third thing, namely (3) *what we think about it*; and in speech, besides what we talk about, there is what we say about it. It is sometimes said by grammarians that the subject of a sentence indicates what we are talking about, and the predicate is or indicates what we say about it (or of it), though as Cook Wilson has pointed out,[2] this is not quite right. If we say (or think) that grass is green, we do not say that what we say (or think) about grass is the predicate *is green*, but rather that what we say or think about it is *that it is green*. (1), what we say or think (in this case, *that grass is green*), is more like (3) than

---

[1] G. Ryle, 'Are There Propositions?', *Proceedings of the Aristotelian Society*, 30 (1929–30), 91–126.
[2] J. Cook Wilson, *Statement and Inference*, Part II, Ch. IV, § 55, pp. 114–17.

like (2), though (3) and (1) are not the same, as Cook Wilson suggests that they are; and perhaps this is why it is not quite natural to call (1) an *object* of speech or thought ('that it is green' doesn't sound a bit like a name of an object; and 'that grass is green' not much more so). However, we shall, in the meantime, go on calling it that. And for our provisional justification, we may notice another thing that Cook Wilson says, namely that while we say that 'is green' is the predicate of the sentence 'Grass is green', what is commonly said to be *predicated of* grass in this sentence is not this but *greenness*. This does sound like some sort of object, and yet 'greenness' and the phrase 'that it is green' are sometimes interchangeable. We say both 'That it is green, is predicated of grass in this sentence', and 'Greenness is predicated of grass in it'. And rather similarly, we may sometimes interchange 'That grass is green' and 'The greenness of grass', as in 'That grass is green is unknown to (or denied by) the Eskimos'. In 'The greenness of grass is more intense than that of gum-leaves' we have a quite different usage, a particular quality of greenness being meant rather than the fact that grass is green; 'the greenness of grass' in this sense cannot be asserted or denied, any more than the fact that grass is green can be intense. But 'the greenness of grass' in the sense in which we may assert or deny it (as opposed to asserting or denying it *of*, say, gum-leaves), is an object of thought in our sense (1), and to believe *in* the greenness of grass in this sense is just to believe *that* grass is green.

2. *Facts and propositions. What we think,* may be *false*; and what we think *about,* may be *non-existent.* These are quite different defects, though philosophers have sometimes slipped into treating them as if they were the same. The philosophical problems raised by the fact that what we think *about* may be *non-existent,* are serious and vexing ones, and they will constitute the main topic of Part II; but those raised by the fact that *what we think* may be *false* are in themselves insignificant, and will *not* constitute the main topic of Part I; though in both Parts we shall from time to time need to remind ourselves of this latter fact (that what we think may be false). For example, in considering the theory that when we think *that some men are beasts* the men we are thinking about are those who are in fact beasts, it is useful to

remind ourselves that we could think that some men are beasts when in fact no men are.[1]

The central philosophical problem about 'objects of thought' in sense (1) is of a different order. What we think *about*, at all events what we ostensibly think about, is *sometimes* abstract, e.g. we may think about numbers, or redness, or the fact that grass is green. But *what we think* is *always* abstract; and equally so whether it be false or true. *That grass is green* is no less abstract, and to that extent no more 'real', than *that grass is pink*. We may, and do, say that *that grass is green* is a *fact*, and that *that grass is pink* is not; but this is to say no more than that grass *is* green and is *not* pink. There are no *serious* problems that *false* thoughts present which *true* thoughts do not present also.

It has sometimes been said that 'facts' are neither more nor less than *true propositions*.[2] Are they? Yes; so long as what this means is not that facts are true *sentences*, but that facts and true propositions alike are mere 'logical constructions' (what this precisely means we shall examine shortly), and that they are the *same* 'logical constructions' (to have 'true propositions' *and* 'facts' is to have *too many* logical constructions). 'What we think is a fact' certainly means no more and no less than 'What we think is true'; and this identity of meaning remains whether we use this pair of expressions as complete sentences or as mere parts of sentences (e.g. 'What we think is a fact is not always so' means the same as 'What we think is true is not always so'). Usage sometimes resists the replacement of 'true proposition' by 'fact', or vice versa, but the grounds of this resistance are usually trivial. In the elementary case, 'That *p* is a true proposition' always = 'That *p* is a fact' ('That grass is green is a true proposition' = 'That grass is green is a fact'). Maybe 'proposition' *feels* more as if it requires an actual 'propounding', but this is surely because of the *other* meaning of 'proposition' ('sentence'). But 'Fact = true proposition' is wrong if it means that facts are tied to propounding too. *That the sun is hot* was a fact before anyone said so (or thought so); but it was a true proposition before then too. Moore has an excellent argument for this. 'That the sun is hot is a true proposition' = 'That the sun is hot is a

[1] Cf. P. T. Geach, *Reference and Generality*, pp. 6–7.
[2] Cf. J. M. Shorter, 'Facts, Logical Atomism and Reducibility', *Australasian Journal of Philosophy*, 40. 3 (Dec. 1962), 283–302.

fact', because both = the plain 'The sun is hot'; and the sun was hot before anyone said so (or thought so); *ergo*, etc.

But equally, *that the sun is cold* was a falsehood (was false; was a false proposition) before anyone propounded or believed this falsehood: for 'That the sun is cold, is false' = 'The sun is not cold', and before there were any thoughts, or sayings, the sun was not cold; *ergo*, etc.[1]

3. *The 'realist' theory of propositions.* Moore's argument is exciting, because it draws a realist conclusion from a positivist premiss. And this is a good point at which to take stock of the polemical ramifications of the truisms so far enunciated. It is easy to see that our thinking or saying is one thing, and what we think or say another (there may be different thinkings or sayings of the same thing); and also that the sentences by which we say things are different from what we say by them (for we may say the same thing by different sentences, e.g. in different languages); and again, what we think or say is obviously different from what we think or speak *about*. From these facts the early Moore and Russell drew the conclusion that the furniture of the universe includes, besides thinkings, sayings, sentences, and the things (grass, etc.) that we think or speak about, further objects, of an abstract sort, which they called 'propositions', of which some had (independently of our beliefs and assertions) the property truth, and others the property falsehood.[2] 'Facts' also seemed to be necessary, since a true proposition is one which accords with a fact and a false proposition one which discords with one.

This is 'realism'. Moore and Russell did not invent this theory. It is well known to have been anticipated, for example, by Bolzano, in his references to the 'proposition in itself' or 'sentence in itself' (*Satz an sich*—the phrase is obviously an adaptation of the *Ding an sich*, 'thing in itself', of Kant), by which he meant 'any statement whatever to the effect that something is or is not, irrespective of whether the statement be true or false, irrespective of whether any person ever formulated it in words, and even irrespective of whether it ever entered any mind as a thought'.[3] What is here in question is admitted to be a 'state-

---

[1] *The Commonplace Book of G. E. Moore*, p. 375.

[2] G. E. Moore, *Some Main Problems of Philosophy*, Ch. III.

[3] Quoted and translated in D. A. Steele's 'Historical Introduction' to the English translation of Bolzano's *Paradoxes of the Infinite*, p. 45.

ment' (*Aussage*), but this is plainly understood neither as a stating nor as the words in which we state a thing, but as the thing stated in these words, which thing may also exist unstated and unthought of. There is a hint of such entities even in J. S. Mill. For Mill, 'proposition' means sentence, but he insists that what a 'proposition' (in this sense) 'puts into words' is not just a belief or disbelief, but 'whatever can be the object' of a belief or disbelief,[1] and he insists that no adequate account can be given either of sentences or of beliefs and disbeliefs unless we distinguish between 'the state of mind called Belief' and 'what is believed', between the 'fact of entertaining' a 'doctrine or opinion' and the doctrine or opinion entertained, between 'assent' and 'what is assented to'. It is to this 'objective' factor— 'not . . . the act of believing, but . . . the thing believed'—that he refers throughout when he asks the series of questions, 'What is the immediate object of belief in a Proposition? What is the matter of fact signified by it? What is it to which, when I assert the proposition, I give my assent, and call upon others to give theirs? What is that which is expressed by the form of discourse called a Proposition, and the conformity of which to fact consti- tutes the truth of that proposition?'[2]

4. *The multiple relation theory of believing.* In another version of realism, Meinong's, propositions were called 'objectives', and facts made a privileged sub-class of these.[3] 'Facts are true propo- sitions' is, as far as it goes, a Meinongian thesis; and is, as far as it goes, a simplification, since it cuts down this type of abstract object from three sub-types to two; but many have felt that this still leaves us with plenty.

These many included, later, Russell and Moore, but they were, to begin with, half-hearted. They dismissed 'objective falsehoods', but kept facts. Russell's name is associated with two variants of this position; in one, the important difference is between knowledge and belief; in the other, between true beliefs and false ones. According to the first theory (the 'mul- tiple relation' theory) knowledge is always of facts, and is a relation between two genuine objects, the knower and the fact known; but belief is not a two-termed relation between the

---

[1] *System of Logic*, i. i. 2.      [2] Ibid. i. v. i.
[3] See J. N. Findlay, *Meinong's Theory of Objects and Values*, pp. 87–8.

believer and the fact or falsehood believed, but a many-termed relation between the believer and the several elements of what would be (if there were such a thing) the proposition believed; and if there is a fact in which these elements are 'knit together' in a way that corresponds (in a rather obscure sense) to their knitting together in the belief, the belief is true; if not, not. Thus Othello's belief that Desdemona loves Cassio knits together the terms Othello, Desdemona, loving, and Cassio in an order that may be represented by

Believes (Othello, loving, Desdemona, Cassio);

and if there were a fact that could be represented by

Loves (Desdemona, Cassio),

i.e. if it were a fact that Desdemona loved Cassio, Othello's belief would be true, but since there is no such fact, it is false.[1]

'Propositions are logical constructions' was first said as a summing-up of this theory.[2] It meant that statements which appear to be about people and propositions are really about people and quite other things, so that it is not necessary to suppose that there really are such things as propositions. Taking a slightly simpler example than Russell's, 'Othello believes that Desdemona is unfaithful', or 'Othello believes in the unfaithfulness of Desdemona', appears to express a relation between Othello and a more abstract object designated by the noun clause 'that Desdemona is unfaithful', or by the phrase 'the unfaithfulness of Desdemona', but it cannot really express any such relation because there is just no such thing as the unfaithfulness of Desdemona, since she is *not* unfaithful. But if we rephrase the statement as 'Othello ascribes infidelity to Desdemona', this appearance vanishes, and it is seen that the statement is not about the infidelity of Desdemona at all, but about the two real objects Desdemona and infidelity, to which Othello stands in the complex relation of ascribing the latter to the former. And all statements which appear to be about

---

[1] Russell, *Problems of Philosophy*, Ch. 12.

[2] More accurately, it is said in the Introduction to *Principia Mathematica* that propositions are 'incomplete symbols'. But Russell's use, in the second decade of this century, of the phrases 'incomplete symbol', 'logical construction', and 'logical fiction', is a chaos into which we need not here enter. Our use is substantially the tidied-up usage of John Wisdom's articles on 'Logical Constructions' in *Mind*, 1931–3.

propositions can be so paraphrased that this appearance vanishes; in this sense, 'propositions are logical constructions'.

Propositions *are* logical constructions, but not, I think, for these reasons. For (1), although Russell's theory does not ask us to believe that there is such an object as the infidelity of Desdemona, it still asks us to believe that there is, over and above Desdemona herself, such an object as her fidelity (the 'fact' of her fidelity), and also that there is such an object as infidelity *tout court*, i.e. the 'universal' Infidelity. Also (2), in this example believing is a three-termed relation but in Russell's own example it is four-termed, and in general the sort of relation that believing is will depend on what it is that is being believed. Russell himself, following Wittgenstein, came to accept the first objection, or at least that part of it which concerns the universal Infidelity (or Loving, in his own example). Sentences describing beliefs, he said at this later stage, are sentences with two verbs, and to bring out their logical structure the subordinate verb as well as the principal one should occur as a verb, not swallowed up in a pseudo-name (abstract noun).[1] I would put it thus: 1. 'Othello ascribes infidelity to Desdemona' = 2. 'Othello believes that Desdemona is unfaithful'; but if we are to *explain* anything by adverting to this identity of meaning, we explain 1 by saying that it simply means 2, rather than vice versa, since it is precisely the apparent reference in 1 to an abstract object called Infidelity which *needs* explaining. Propositions aren't the *only* logical constructions that need to be shown to be such by being paraphrased away, and in giving us 1 for 2 Russell is offering us a poor metaphysical bargain, which only a too one-eyed concentration on the matter in hand ('propositions') could persuade anyone to accept.[2]

There is also an objection, due to F. P. Ramsey,[3] to that part of Russell's theory which asserts that, even though belief is *not*, knowledge or perception *is*, a relation between a person and a fact. For suppose that X believes that Y perceives that a certain knife is to the left of a certain book; but suppose that in fact Y

---

[1] Russell, 'The Philosophy of Logical Atomism' (1918), IV (in *Logic and Knowledge*, p. 226).

[2] Russell is in fact guilty of the same combination of scepticism at the centre with dogmatism at the periphery of attention which H. H. Price has detected in Hume. (*Hume's Theory of the External World*, pp. 17–18.)

[3] *Foundations of Mathematics*, p. 140.

does not and cannot perceive this simply because it is not true, and the knife is in fact to the right of the book. On the Russellian analysis, X's belief would consist in a four-termed relation between X, Y, perceiving, and the fact that the knife is to the left of the book; but *ex hypothesi* there is no such fact. X's belief *could* consist in such a four-termed relation if it were true, or if it were true that the knife is to the left of the book, but what a belief consists in surely cannot depend in this way upon what is true; indeed, one of the main motivations of Russell's theory is to give an account of belief which doesn't make what is believed depend on the belief's truth or falsehood.

5. *Beliefs as pointers to facts.* In Russell's other theory,[1] in which the important distinction is not that between belief and perception (or knowledge), but that between true and false beliefs, Meinong's word 'objective' is misused to denote the one fact which makes a given belief true or false as the case may be. True and false beliefs alike are said to have facts as their 'objectives', but the true ones hit the mark and the false ones miss it. 'Grass is green' and 'Grass is not green' alike 'correspond', in a broad sense, to the fact that grass is green, but the correspondence in the one case is an accordance with (a 'pointing towards') this fact, in the other case a discordance with (a 'pointing away from') the same fact. Basically the theory is Wittgenstein's; propositions (i.e. sentences) are 'pictures of facts' which may represent or misrepresent the facts they depict, and this representation or misrepresentation is the 'sense' of the proposition. Here belief, whether true or false, *does* consist in a relation to a fact, only it is a different relation in the two cases.

This theory, however, either gives no account at all of *what is believed,* or else makes this something different when the belief is false and when it is true. When I believe, for example, that Jones is musical, what I believe is the fact that Jones is musical, if that *is* a fact; but if it is not a fact, what I believe, when I believe that Jones is musical, is the fact that Jones is *not* musical, only I somehow don't believe this the right way. This is quite incredible, and is probably not what Russell is actually saying,

[1] Adumbrated in his 1918 lectures on 'The Philosophy of Logical Atomism' (reproduced in *Logic and Knowledge*), and in *The Analysis of Mind,* pp. 271–3.

but in that case the theory gives no account at all of what it is that goes on when I have this belief whether it is true or false. It might be suggested that A believes that grass is green if and only if either grass is green and A mentally points towards the fact that grass is green, or grass is not green and A mentally points away from the fact that grass is not green.[1] But if we neutral observers, in believing that A believes that grass is green, are supposed to be entertaining this disjunction, what are *we* supposed to be relating ourselves to in entertaining that part of it which concerns a fact which is non-existent?

6. *The 'No truth' theory.* This last objection also is substantially F. P. Ramsey's, but what is chiefly important about Ramsey is his own alternative theory. For Ramsey, 'propositions are logical constructions' in a new way; and what is all-important, facts for Ramsey are logical constructions too. The basic contexts in which we appear to be talking about propositions and facts are ones in which we ascribe truth or falsehood to the former, and here the elimination of these apparent objects or subjects of discourse is easy. 'That grass is green is a true proposition' = 'The proposition that grass is green is a true one' = 'That grass is green is a truth' = 'That grass is green is a fact' = 'It is a fact that grass is green' = 'It is true that grass is green' = 'It is the case that grass is green' = the plain 'Grass is green'. And 'That grass is green is a false proposition' = 'The proposition that grass is green is a false one' = 'That grass is green is a falsehood' = 'It is false that grass is green' = 'It is not the case that grass is green' = 'Grass is not green'.[2] How we can handle 'proposition' and 'fact' in other contexts than these elementary ones, is a matter to be looked into later, but we now have at least a beginning.

Ramsey's is sometimes called the 'No truth' theory of truth, but its final upshot is not sceptical. To say that sentences containing the words 'proposition' and 'fact' mean no more and no less than sentences which do not contain either these words or other words or phrases equivalent to them, is not to say that such sentences ought not to be used, or are meaningless; on the contrary, it is to say what their meaning is. Ramsey's theory in

[1] I owe this suggestion to Professor Richard Montague.
[2] F. P. Ramsey, *Foundations of Mathematics*, pp. 142–3.

fact preserves all that is obviously true in the others, even in the 'realist' ones. We have already seen that it preserves, and even supplies a particularly conclusive way of defending, the truth that truths and falsehoods are such independently of what we think or say, and indeed of whether there is anyone to do any thinking or saying. Here we come back to Moore's argument. Moore seems in the end to have accepted Ramsey's basic reductions, but he used them to establish one of his own earliest points. If 'The proposition that the sun is hot is true' and 'That the sun is hot is a fact' just mean 'The sun is hot', they *must* be, precisely because of this, mind-independent and language-independent, for the sun's being hot in no way depends on anyone's thinking or saying that it is.

'Propositions (facts) are logical constructions' is a saying that can be easily misconstrued. Because it is at bottom a statement about linguistic entities, it is thought to mean that propositions (facts) are themselves linguistic entities, e.g. sentences. If propositions were sentences, they *wouldn't* be logical constructions, for sentences are not logical constructions; or at all events 'sentences' in the sense of particular inscriptions are not logical constructions, but perfectly ordinary objects. 'Propositions are logical constructions' is an assertion about language, but it isn't an assertion that propositions are themselves bits of language, but rather an assertion about sentences that are ostensibly about propositions, to the effect that they are not in reality about propositions but about something else. This is what 'Propositions are logical constructions' means whether it is expanded, as at first, in terms of Russell's multiple-relation theory or, as now, in terms of Ramsey's theory. Part of what it says may be, e.g. that the sentence 'The proposition that the sun is hot is true' means no more and no less than the sentence 'The sun is hot', i.e. the sentence 'The proposition that the sun is hot is true' is not in reality about the proposition that the sun is hot, but about the sun. Similarly 'The proposition that the sun is hot would be true even if unasserted' means the same as 'The sun would be hot even if no one said so', and is not about the proposition that the sun is hot but about the sun. Propositions, and their truth and falsehood, are language-independent just *because* propositions are logical constructions, or at least because they are logical constructions of this particular sort.

Note that the sentence 'The sentence $S$ is only ostensibly and not in reality about propositions' is itself only ostensibly and not in reality about propositions. There is nothing viciously circular about this. Just as 'The proposition that $p$ is true' and 'The proposition that $p$ is false' can be so rephrased that the quasi-designation 'The proposition that $p$' disappears, so can 'The sentence $S$ is only ostensibly about the proposition that $p$' be so rephrased that the quasi-designation that forms its grammatical *object* disappears, and along with it the transitive verb 'is only ostensibly about' which governs it.

# 2

## PROPOSITIONS AND SENTENCES

1. *Beliefs and forms of words.* We began with propositions and
facts as objects of thought, but slipped perhaps too easily into
discussing propositions as the vehicles of truth and falsehood,
and facts as true propositions. It is by no means clear that considerations which illuminate our ascriptions of truth and falsity
to propositions will equally illuminate our use of noun clauses
beginning with 'that' to express what we think as distinct from
our thinking it.[1] Indeed, is anything left of this distinction at all
if what are ostensibly designations of propositions are paraphrased away as in the last chapter?

Let us begin by examining an obvious error, namely the error
that whenever we think something, what we think is a sentence.
It is, I hope, obvious that this *is* an error. It is less obviously an
error to say that whenever we *say* something, what we say is a
sentence. For in saying something we do, in general, utter sentences, and it may well seem a mere verbal idiosyncrasy, of no
philosophical importance, that while we do speak of 'uttering'
sentences we don't generally speak of 'saying' them. It seems
clear, nevertheless, that we can say the same thing by uttering
different sentences, and that in telling someone what somebody
said (e.g. that he said that grass is green) we do not *ipso facto* tell
him what sentence he uttered, but only tell him something
which perhaps entails that he uttered *a* sentence. It is at all
events clear as regards *thinking* that even if we do always think
*in* sentences, we do not think sentences. It is even more clear
that we do not fear, hope, desire, etc., sentences. Or at least the
objects of such fears, hopes, etc., as are expressed by saying that
someones fears *that* so-and-so, hopes *that* so-and-so, desires *that*
so-and-so, are not sentences. A man might perhaps in some odd
mood or condition fear sentences as he fears dogs—if Robinson

---

[1] Cf. R. Cartwright, 'Propositions', in *Analytical Philosophy* (ed. R. J. Butler), 1st
series, pp. 81–103.

Crusoe had seen not a footstep but the inscription 'The cat is on the mat' written in the sand, it might have set him trembling— but this is quite a different matter; such a man might fear the sentence without knowing what it means; and even if he did, he might fear the sentence 'The cat is on the mat' without fearing that the cat is on the mat. And to fear that the cat is on the mat is not itself to fear this sentence.

One might well argue, nevertheless, that although fearing that *p*, thinking that *p*, etc., do not amount to fearing, thinking, etc., a sentence which means that *p*, they do amount to doing *other* things to, or standing in other relations to, such a sentence, much as saying that *p* amounts to, or at least in some sense involves, *uttering* such a sentence. And it is indeed true, even trivially true, that whoever fears, thinks, etc., that *p*, *ipso facto* stands in *a* relation to such a sentence. For to fear that I am going off my head is *ipso facto* to fear that which I might assert by uttering the sentence 'I am going off my head'; and this does constitute a complicated relation between me and this sentence.

This concession is, however, a trivial one. For it is equally true that, although *breaking one's leg* is quite obviously not a relation between a person and any form of words whatever, and to break my leg is certainly not to break the phrase 'my leg', nevertheless in breaking my leg I do *ipso facto* stand in *a* relation to this phrase, since in breaking my leg I break something which would normally be described in English by this phrase. Breaking one's leg, all the same, does not *consist in* standing in this relation to this phrase, and 'I have broken my leg' does not *mean* 'I have broken what would normally be called in English "my leg"'; I could as easily break my leg if no such phrase existed, or if its use in English were quite different from what it is; and it is in some sense *because* I have broken my leg that I stand in this relation to this phrase, not vice versa, i.e. my relation to the phrase is *parasitic upon* my relation to my leg.

Almost all of these considerations apply, *mutatis mutandis*, to fearing, thinking, etc. Whoever fears or thinks that there will be a nuclear war, although he does not fear the sentence 'There will be a nuclear war', does stand in *a* relation to this sentence, since he fears that something is the case which could be asserted by uttering this sentence. But his fear does not *consist in* this relation to this sentence; 'X fears that there will be a nuclear

war' does not *mean* 'X fears that something is the case which
could be asserted by uttering the sentence "There will be a
nuclear war"'; a man could have this fear if no such sentence
existed, or if it meant something quite different from what it
does; and it is *because* he fears that there will be a nuclear war
that he stands in this relation to this sentence, rather than vice
versa, i.e. his relation to the sentence is parasitic—but here we
are brought to a halt. His relation to the sentence is parasitic
upon his relation to *what?* In the other case we could say that
my relation to the phrase 'my leg' is parasitic upon my relation
to my leg, i.e. to what the phrase designates. But we cannot say
that the man's relation to the sentence 'There will be a nuclear
war' is parasitic upon his relation to what this sentence designates. Certainly it is parasitic upon his fear that there will be a
nuclear war, but this fear is not a relation to what the sentence
'There will be a nuclear war' designates, for designating objects
is just not what sentences do.

We can say, if we like, that 'X fears that there will be a nuclear
war' expresses X's relation to *the proposition that* there will be a
nuclear war, i.e. to the proposition which the sentence 'There
will be a nuclear war' expresses (even if it doesn't 'designate' it).
But even if a philosophical theory might lead us to say this, it is
in fact unusual for people to say 'X fears the proposition that
so-and-so', or even 'X thinks the proposition that so-and-so'.
I am not sure what is the reason for this; we do say 'X fears
(thinks) that so-and-so', and we do say 'That so-and-so, is a
proposition', and yet we do not say 'X fears a proposition'.
I suspect that we treat propositions as entities when we feel we
have to, otherwise not; and in reality we *never* have to.

2. *The grammar of believing.* What we must get away from, I suspect, is the whole idea that 'X fears (thinks) that there will be
a nuclear war' *has* to express a relation between X and anything
whatever. And we cannot get away from this idea without
adverting to the difference between a name (or other designation) and a sentence. We do not fear, hope, desire, or think
sentences—we must stick fast to that. And fearing, hoping,
desiring, and thinking do not *consist in* relations between people
and sentences—'X fears (thinks) that *p*' does not *mean* that X
stands in some relation to some sentence by which we would

ordinarily assert that *p*—we must stick fast to that too. Nevertheless, if we are to bring out the difference between *what X thinks* when X thinks that there will be a nuclear war, and *what X breaks* when X breaks his leg—the difference, if you like, between 'objects of thought', in sense (1), and 'objects of breaking'—we do have to talk about sentences, we do have to engage in 'linguistic analysis'. We are, after all, still commenting on the dictum that 'propositions are logical constructions', and it has already been admitted that this is a statement about language, even if it is *not* the statement that a proposition (in the sense of what we think, or what is true or false) is itself a bit of language.

In at least most languages, there are sentences, and there are names, and there are ways of forming sentences from names, and ways of forming sentences from other sentences. If we form a sentence from a name by attaching another expression to it, we call this expression a *verb* or verb-phrase; in formal logic we call it a predicate. Only names designate objects; sentences do not, and verbs do not. A sentence can express what we think; a name can designate what we are thinking about; and a verb can express what we think about that thing. If we form a sentence from two names by attaching an expression to them (usually, but not necessarily, between them), we call that expression a transitive verb or verb-phrase; in formal logic we call it a 'two-place' predicate. (There are also three-place predicates, four-place predicates, etc., as we saw when considering Russell's 'multiple relation' theory of believing, but we need not at present concern ourselves with these.) And we may say that a two-place predicate expresses a *relation* between the objects designated by the names to which it is attached. For example, in 'I broke my leg', the two-place predicate 'broke' expresses a relation between me and my leg. If a sentence is formed from one or more names, it may be said to be *about* the objects designated by these names. For example 'I broke my leg' is about me, and is also about my leg. There are certain vaguenesses and over-simplifications in this story which will need to be remedied in Part II, but they do not affect the business now in hand.

If we form a sentence from two other sentences by attaching an expression to them (usually, but not necessarily, between them), we call that expression a conjunction; in formal logic we call it a connective. Connectives are not predicates, and do not express relations. For example, in 'Grass is green and the sky is blue', 'and' is not a predicate, and does not express a relation, either between the sentences 'Grass is green' and 'The sky is blue', or between any other objects or entities. Nor is the compound sentence *about* its component sentences, or about the propositions expressed by them, if such there be. Certainly 1. 'Grass is green and the sky is blue' means the same as 2. 'The propositions that grass is green and that the sky is blue are both true', but 2 does not 'explain' the meaning of 1; rather, 1 explains the meaning of 2 (cf. Chapter 1). However, 1 is not about nothing, and does contain an expression which signifies a relation between the things it is about, though 'and' is not this expression. For if the components of a compound sentence contain names, and are thus about objects, the compound sentence obviously also contains these names, and is about these objects. 'Grass is green and the sky is blue', for example, is about grass, and about the sky, and says of them that the former is green and the latter blue, and this *does* constitute a relation between them, expressed not by the conjunction 'and' but by the two-place predicate '— is green and — is blue'. (The relation expressed is one of colour-contrast.)

But these do not by any means exhaust the ways in which sentences may be formed. In particular, a sentence may be formed from two other expressions of which one is a name and one is a sentence; where this is done by attaching an expression to the name on the one hand and the component sentence on the other, there is no stock technical term of grammar or logic to describe such expressions, but they exist nevertheless. For example, the sentence 'Grass is green and the sky is blue' *could* be thought of as formed from the noun 'grass' and the component sentence 'the sky is blue' by placing between them the expression '— is green and —'. This sequence of words no more expresses a relation between grass and something else than the conjunction 'and' does, though like the conjunction 'and' it is a component of the two-place predicate '— is green and — is blue', which does express a relation between grass and the sky.

To analyse the sentence 'Grass is green and the sky is blue' as consisting of the noun 'grass', the sentence 'the sky is blue', and the unchristened link '— is green and —' is a little odd, and is not in itself very illuminating; but when we come to 'X fears (thinks) that there will be a nuclear war', the possibilities which it suggests are important. For expressions like '— fears that —' and '— thinks that —' have precisely this function of forming sentences from other expressions of which the first is a name and the second another sentence. They are as it were predicates at one end and connectives at the other. They do not express relations between the object designated by the name attached at the left and the object designated by the name attached at the right, because what is attached at the right *isn't* a name but a sentence, and so doesn't designate anything whatever. So we eliminate the apparent name 'that there will be a nuclear war', and the suggestion it carries that the complete sentence expresses a relation between X and the 'proposition' designated by this name, simply by ceasing to parse the whole as 'X fears / that there will be a nuclear war', and parsing it instead as 'X fears that / there will be a nuclear war'.[1]

This solution is not different in principle from Ramsey's elimination of 'The proposition that *p*' from 'The proposition that *p* is true' and 'The proposition that *p* is false'. Phrases such as 'fears that' and 'thinks that' are predicates at the left and connectives at the right, in the quite precise sense that if the right-hand gap is filled in by an actual sentence what remains with a left-hand gap is simply a one-place predicate (e.g. '— fears that there will be a nuclear war'), while if the left-hand gap is filled by an actual name what remains with a right-hand gap is precisely a one-place connective (to employ a reasonable logical barbarism), 'X believes that —'. This expression is of the same logical type as 'It is not the case that —', which remains after Ramsey's elimination of the quasi-verb 'is false'. 'The proposition that grass is pink is false' means no more and no less than 'It is not the case that / grass is pink' or 'Grass is not pink', which is not, and does not even look like, a sentence about the proposition that grass is pink, but looks like, and is, a slightly more complicated sentence about grass. Similarly 'The proposition that grass is pink is believed by X' means no more and no less than 'X believes that / grass is pink', or 'Grass is, in X's opinion, pink', which again is not, and does not even look like, a sentence about the proposition that grass is pink, but looks

*NB.*

[1] Cf. A. N. Prior, 'Oratio Obliqua', *Proceedings of the Aristotelian Society*, Suppl. 37 (1963), 115–26.

like, and is, a slightly more complicated sentence about grass (and also about X). The alternative renderings, incidentally, make it clear that in ordinary grammar what the logician calls a one-place connective is an adverb or adverbial phrase. There are again some over-simplifications in this account which will require correction, or at least discussion, in Part II; but the main point is clear.

This method of dispensing with 'propositions' in belief contexts has been advocated, a little hesitantly, by W. V. O. Quine. After toying with the use of square brackets to transform sentences into 'that' clauses, which name the 'objects' of 'propositional attitudes', Quine decides that we can do without these after all. 'We can continue to formulate the propositional attitudes with help of the notations of intensional abstraction . . . but just cease to view these notations as singular terms referring to objects. This means viewing "Tom believes [Cicero denounced Catiline]" no longer as of the form "$Fab$" with $a =$ Tom and $b =$ [Cicero denounced Catiline], but rather as of the form "$Fa$" with $a =$ Tom and complex "$F$". The verb "believes" here ceases to be a term and becomes part of an operator "believes that", or "believes [  ]", which, applied to a sentence, produces a composite absolute general term whereof the sentence is counted an immediate constituent.'[1] This is precisely my own proposal; it is one of the two points in the philosophy of logic on which Quine seems to me dead right.

The sort of bother that this move puts an end to may be illustrated by a passage in which Ramsey's theory of truth was anticipated by W. E. Johnson, who compared the vacuity of 'truly' with multiplication by unity.[2] Johnson's exposition, so admirable at this point, is spoilt by occurring in the context of a needless worry about whether 'true' and 'false' construct what he calls 'secondary' propositions, i.e. propositions about other propositions (in the sense of abstract entities). Precisely because he was aware that the proposition that the proposition that $p$ is true is identical with the plain proposition that $p$, he could not take the former seriously as a 'secondary' proposition, but he did feel that the assertion of a proposition's falsehood, like that of its necessity or contingency, or of its being asserted by someone, had to be so classified. This, however, seemed to jeopardize the

---

[1] W. V. O. Quine, *Word and Object*, p. 216.    [2] *Logic*, I. iv. 1–2.

identification of '*p*-false' with 'not-*p*', since it seems reasonable to regard 'not' as coming out of the same box as 'and', and '*p*-and-*q*', with the separate propositions primary, isn't a secondary proposition but a compound primary. This in turn led Johnson to confine 'primary' negation to some affection of the subject-predicate relation 'within' the (primary) proposition. What needs to be said to all this is surely that the case which Johnson found so problematic is the one clear case which gives the key to all the others. They are *none* of them 'about' the proposition that *p*, and *all* of them about whatever that proposition is about.

3. *Truth and correspondence.* We can now give an account of truth and falsehood as applied not merely to propositions, i.e. to what we believe or assert, but also as applied to particular believings and assertings. 'X's belief (assertion) that there will be a nuclear war is true' means no more and no less than 'X believes (says) that there will be a nuclear war, and there *will* be one', while 'X's belief (assertion) that there will be a nuclear war is false' means no more and no less than 'X believes (says) that there will be a nuclear war, but there won't be one'. Justified and unjustified hopes and fears can be similarly dealt with.

It is at this point that it is appropriate to associate the notion of truth with that of 'correspondence' or 'conformity' with fact. I do not know when the term 'correspondence' was first used in this connection, but *correspondentia* is already to be found in Aquinas's *De Veritate*. Goodness, he says, consists in a certain *convenientia* or conformity with desire (*appetitus*), and truth in a similar *convenientia* with the intellect. The first essential here is that being should correspond with the intellect (*ut ens intellectui correspondeat*), and this *correspondentia* is called *adaequatio rei et intellectus*. This last phrase, which Aquinas attributes to the tenth-century Jewish Neo-platonist Isaac Israeli, is what he finally settles on as his definition of truth, and he expands it by referring to Aristotle's remark in the *Metaphysics* that 'To say of what is that it is not, or of what is not that it is, is false, while to say of what is that it is, and of what is not that it is not, is true.'[1] The contemporary *locus classicus* for the theory is perhaps the fifteenth chapter of G. E. Moore's *Some Main Problems of*

[1] *Met.* 1011ᵇ26 ff.; Aquinas, *De Veritate*, Q.1, A.1.

*Philosophy*. Moore supposes some friend of his to believe mistakenly that he has gone away for his holidays, and remarks:

> We should, I think, certainly say . . . that if this belief of his is *true* then I *must* have gone away for my holidays; . . . and conversely, we should also say that *if* I *have* gone away, then this belief of his certainly *is* true.

So far, this is entirely Aristotelian. Moore goes on to say, however, that although his being away is a 'necessary and sufficient condition' of the truth of his friend's belief, it cannot be what is *meant* by this belief's being true. For

> when we assert: 'The belief that I have gone away is true', we mean to assert that this belief has some property, which it shares with other true beliefs. . . . But in merely asserting 'I have gone away', we are not attributing any property at all to this belief. . . . We are merely asserting a fact, which might quite well be a fact, even if no one believed it at all. Plainly I might have gone away, without my friend believing that I had; and if so, his belief would not be true, because it would not exist.

Moore is driven by these conclusions to the position that the truth of a belief consists in its standing to a fact in a relation which is not definable but which is 'perfectly familiar', and is, in the given case, 'expressed by the circumstance that the name of the belief is "The belief that I have gone away" while the name of the fact' (to which, if true, it is related) 'is "That I have gone away"'. This relation he calls 'correspondence'.

It seems doubtful whether Moore held this view at a later stage; at all events, his argument here is muddled. In the first place, the reason he gives for denying that his actually having gone away would *constitute* the truth of his friend's belief that he had, is equally a reason for denying that the former is a 'sufficient condition' of the latter (as Moore says it is). And secondly, if we make the obvious correction to give us what really *would* be a sufficient condition, the same correction would give us a definition also. His friend's belief that he has gone away is true if and only if *his friend believes that he has*, and he has. And more generally, to say that X's belief that $p$ is true is to say that X believes that $p$ and (it is the case that) $p$. There seems no reason to see any more in 'correspondence with fact' than this.

In the 1950s the defence of a form of the correspondence theory by J. L. Austin gave rise to a curious controversy with P. F. Strawson about whether or not 'facts' are 'in the world'. Austin maintained that 'if there is to be communication of the sort that we achieve by language at all, there must be' not only 'a stock of symbols of some kind', which may be called the 'words', but also 'something other than the words, which the words are to be used to communicate about', which may be called the 'world'. And 'when a statement is true, there is . . . a state of affairs which makes it true and which is *toto mundo* distinct from the true statement about it'.[1] Strawson, opposing this, insists that the only things 'in the world' with which our statements are connected are the objects that they are 'about', and that facts are not among these. 'Facts are what statements (when true) state; they are not what statements are about.' 'The only plausible candidate for the position of what (in the world) makes the statement true is the fact it states; but the fact it states is not something in the world. It is not an object.'[2]

Part of what Strawson seems to be saying here is that facts are 'logical constructions', and so far, so good. But there seems to be something more, though it is not at all clear what this is. In one particularly flamboyant passage he says:

Of course, statements and facts fit. They were made for each other. If you prise the statements off the world you prise the facts off it too; but the world would be none the poorer.

This is figurative language, and difficult to interpret, but it *seems* to mean that there are no unstated facts, or that if there were no statements there would be no facts, and if this *is* what it means, then (*a*) it is surely false, and (*b*) as we saw in Chapter 1, it by no means follows from the view that facts are logical constructions. And there certainly *is* a tight connection between being a fact and being in the world, though this connection is over-crudely stated if we simply say that facts themselves are 'in the world'.

Phrases like 'in the world', 'genuinely in the world', 'in the real world' get their force from an implied contrast with phrases like 'merely in the mind', 'in the pages of Homer'. The preposition

---

[1] J. L. Austin, *Philosophical Papers*, pp. 89, 91.
[2] *Proceedings of the Aristotelian Society*, Suppl. 24 (1950), 134–7.

'in' suggests a number of boxes in which various sorts of objects may be put, but this suggestion is obviously not to be taken too seriously. To say that something is the case in the pages of Homer is simply to say that Homer says it is the case; to say that God, or trees, exist merely in the mind is to say that it is merely thought that they exist. And to say that something is the case in the real world, or in fact, is simply to drop *all* such qualifying prefixes, and simply say that it is the case. Facts, if you like, *are* the real world (cf. Wittgenstein). And to compare what is said or thought to be the case with what simply *is* the case, is to compare what is the case 'in' our statements or thoughts with what is the case in the world; and the statements or thoughts are true only if what is, in this sense, the case 'in' them is the same as what is the case 'in the world'.

4. *Unspecified beliefs, truths, and falsehoods.* We have now seen how to eliminate what appear to be references to propositions, i.e. to truths (or facts) and falsehoods, from a number of typical contexts, but there is one sort of context from which it does not seem easy to eliminate such references by these methods. For we have so far only considered cases in which the propositions dealt with are actually specified, i.e. in which we have to do with 'the proposition that $p$', and in which the word 'that' occurs in a crucial position. The essential trick is to shift the punctuation or parsing line from before a 'that' to after it (we change 'X thinks / that $p$' to 'X thinks that / $p$'). But how can we do this when no 'that' is present, or no 'that' of the appropriate sort, as in 'Cohen and I always believe (or don't always believe) the same things' (i.e. the same propositions), or 'Some things (i.e. propositions) that Cohen believes, I don't believe', or 'Everything that Cohen says is true (false)'?

Ramsey thought of this one too; his answer to it—the right one, it seems to me—was to move into a slightly more stylized language than ordinary English, with quantifiers binding variables that stand for sentences. We can get our 'that' back where we want it by reading 'I don't believe some of the things that Cohen believes' as 'For some $p$, Cohen believes that $p$, and I do not believe that $p$', and 'Everything that Cohen says is true' as 'For any $p$, if Cohen believes that $p$, then it is the case that $p$', or more briefly 'For any $p$, if Cohen believes that $p$, then $p$'.

Similarly 'There are facts which nobody has ever asserted or ever will assert, but which *are* facts all the same', amounts to 'For some $p$, it never has been and never will be asserted that $p$, but it is the case that $p$ all the same'. We can even give a good sense to 'There are facts' and 'There are falsehoods', and to 'There are falsehoods as well as facts', since these could amount respectively to 'For some $p$, it is the case that $p$' (or simply 'For some $p$, $p$'), 'For some $p$, it is not the case that $p$', and the conjunction of these; but we can give no good sense to 'There are facts and falsehoods as well as things that are neither'. If this means 'For some $p$, it is the case that $p$, and for some $p$, it is not the case that $p$, and for some $p$, it neither is nor is not the case that $p$', it is false (because its last clause is). If it means 'For some $x$, $x$ is a fact, and for some $x$, $x$ is a falsehood, and for some $x$, $x$ is neither a fact nor a falsehood', where '$x$' is the kind of variable that can be replaced by the name of an object, it is nonsense. For 'Percy is a fact' (which would mean 'It is the case that Percy', if it meant anything), 'Percy is a falsehood' (= 'It is not the case that Percy'), 'Percy is neither a fact nor a falsehood' (= 'It neither is nor is not the case that Percy') are all of them senseless, ungrammatical. In what Carnap calls the 'formal mode', i.e. talk about talk, we can of course say truly enough that some expressions are true sentences, some false sentences, and some (e.g. 'Percy') not sentences at all.

This difficulty about 'There are facts and falsehoods as well as things that are neither' can be carried further. I have said, as it were by way of a concession, that we can give a good sense to 'There are facts', 'There are falsehoods', and 'There are propositions'. But can we give any sense to these *but* the 'good' sense—can we give a bad sense to them? Or in other words, can we give a good sense to their denials, i.e. to 'There are no facts', 'There are no falsehoods', 'There are no propositions'? That is, is there any sense in which these last are *true*? If the first, for example, means 'For no $p$ is it a fact that $p$', this is *not* true; but if it means 'For no $x$ is it the case that $x$ is a fact', where '$x$' is the kind of variable that would be instantiated by a name like 'Percy', this isn't true either; but nonsense (since '$x$ is a fact', i.e. 'It is a fact that $x$', is senseless where '$x$' does duty for a name). So what are we arguing about? with whom are we arguing? and what are we trying to say against them? It would seem that the only people who could make sense of 'For no $x$ is it the case that $x$ is a fact' would be our opponents, who would say that it is false. Once again we can fall back on what Carnap calls the 'formal mode', and say, perhaps, that nothing is named by a true sentence, or by a 'that' clause formed from a true sentence; this is, indeed, how we approached this whole matter in the first place, and so far as I can see no other approach is possible. But 'Nothing is named by a true sentence' must be so understood that (*a*) the reason for saying it is different from the reason for saying, e.g. 'Nothing is named by "Pegasus"', and (*b*) it is not meant to exclude such oddities as christening someone 'The-Lord-is-my-shepherd Jones', or someone having (as an eighteenth-century Ghanaian philosopher did have) the surname 'Amo'.

5. *Relations contained in attitude-functions.* It should be noted that expressions like '— believes that —', as well as less natural examples of the same semantical category such as '— is green and —', may occur as parts of two-place predicates even though they are not two-place predicates themselves. Just as '— is green and — is blue' is a two-place predicate expressing a relation that might hold between, say, grass and the sky, so '— believes that — is a Communist' is a two-place predicate expressing a relation that might hold between, say, Paul Jones and Elmer Gantry, i.e. the relation of 'attributing Communism to'. That two-place (and indeed more-place) predicates may be obtained in this way was observed in the 1920s by W. E. Johnson, whose *Logic*[1] contains an instructive survey of some of the possibilities, though his mode of presentation suggests an unnecessary metaphysical 'Platonism'. He points out that we may form a two-place predicate by filling in one of the gaps in an ordinary three-place one, e.g. '— gives — to —' yields '— gives X to —' and 'A gives — to —' (i.e. '— is given by A to —') and '— gives — to B' (i.e. '— is given to B by —'). But where the three-place predicates contain two verbs in them, as in '— prevented — from hurting —', we may not only fill in gaps in such a way as to produce two-place predicates connecting ordinary 'substantival' terms, such as '— prevented B from hurting —', but we may also regroup the components in such a way as to express what John-

---

[1] Part I, Ch. XIII, esp. §§ 7–8.

son describes as a two-place relation between a person and a *possibile*: '— prevented —', where the second gap is filled by something like 'B's hurting C'. If we add an explanatory clause to get something like '— prevented — by instructing —' (e.g. 'A prevented B's hurting C by instructing D') we may regroup again to get a slightly different '— prevented —' which, in Johnson's terminology, relates two *possibilia*, e.g. A's instructing D and B's hurting C. To get all this into the kind of 'logical grammar' recommended here, we would have as an elementary connective (linking two *sentences*) 'That — prevented it from being the case that —', e.g. 'That A instructed D prevented it from being the case that B hurt C', and if the subordinate sentences contain names, we can so make or fill in gaps as to produce (*a*) an expression connecting a name and a sentence, e.g. 'That — instructed D prevented it from being the case that —', or (*b*) an expression connecting two names (i.e. a two-place predicate) e.g. 'That — instructed D prevented it from being the case that B hurt —'; or (*c*) an expression connecting three names (i.e. a three-place predicate), e.g. 'That — instructed D prevented it from being the case that — hurt —'; or (*d*) an expression connecting four names (i.e. a four-place predicate), 'That — instructed — prevented it from being the case that — hurt —'. If we just want to say that A prevented B's hurting C without saying *how* he did so, i.e. if we just want to say that he prevented it *somehow*, we can turn this into our language as 'Something that A did prevented it from being the case that B hurt C', and the new functor involved here, namely

'For some φ, that — φ'd prevented it from being the case that —'

is Johnson's *first* 'prevented', i.e. the 'prevented' that relates a normal term (e.g. A) to a *possibile* (e.g. B's hurting C). Johnson goes on to say that 'asserts that' is a functor of this latter kind, or, as he puts it, from the ordinary dyadic relation expressed by '— asserts — to be P' we can extract the relation between a person and a *possibile* expressed by 'asserts', as in 'A asserts S's being P'; *possibilia*, he says, are from this point of view also *assertibilia*. One might add that *assertibile* seems a better term than *possibile* for what is expressed by a noun clause or phrase, since this may in some cases be an *impossibile*.

The same point is made, in his own way, by Quine.[1] He is concerned with the analysis of sentences like 'Tom believes of Cicero that he denounced Catiline', and his preliminary suggestion is to use the form '$y[y$ denounced Catiline]' for the property of denouncing Catiline, and so to read the whole as 'Tom believes $y[y$ denounced Catiline] of Cicero' ('Tom ascribes having-denounced-Catiline to Cicero'). Then he reinterprets this symbolism as constructing the two-place predicate '— believes $y[y$ denounced Catiline] of —' from the 'open' sentence '$y$ denounced Catiline' by means of the operator '— believes $y[$  ] of —'. I think this amounts to the suggestion that in 'Tom believes that Cicero denounced Catiline' we may not only regard '— believes that —' as constructing the one-place predicate '— believes that Cicero denounced Catiline' out of the sentence (or 'no-place predicate') 'Cicero denounced Catiline' but also as constructing the two-place predicate '— believes that — denounced Catiline' out of the one-place predicate '— denounced Catiline'. But Quine would insist that this is only possible if we read the given sentence in a particular way. If there is a genuine relation between Tom and Cicero which consists in the former's believing of the latter that he denounced Catiline, this relation will equally hold between Tom and Tully, since Tully *is* Cicero; but there is certainly some sense in which Tom, who *ex hypothesi* is unaware of this identity, may believe that Cicero denounced Catiline without believing that Tully did, and so a sense in which he may believe that Cicero denounced Catiline *without* thereby standing in a genuine relation to Cicero (and so to Tully). A similar point may be made about Johnson's 'asserting' example.

The examination of this complication can wait until Part II; but even at this juncture it is worth making the quite general point that while '— asserts that —', '— believes that —', etc. *can* (or apparently can) sometimes function as parts of two-place (or more-place) predicates in this way, they cannot always do so—the possibility of their doing so depends on the presence of a name in the subordinate sentence, and there may not in fact be one there. For example 'A believes that nothing is perfect' doesn't express a relation between A and any object whatever, for no object is named in 'Nothing is perfect'. The functor '—

[1] *Word and Object*, p. 216.

believes that —' occurs here, but the two-place predicate '— believes that — is perfect' does not—it is just not said that A ascribes perfection to anything, nor is it even said (though it is possibly implied) that he does not. For the matter of that, no object is named in 'Something is perfect', and so no relation between A and any object is expressed by 'A believes that something is perfect', at least if this just means that A believes that there is at least one perfect thing, and not that he believes *of* at least one thing that *it* is perfect.

6. *Thinking about abstract objects.* One other apparent gap: it is clear that in some sense we not only *think propositions* but think *about* propositions, i.e. we not only *think that p*, but *think about the proposition that p*. We may think, for example, that the proposition that *p* is a very absurd one, or that it is (or is not) possibly true, or that it was believed by all the ancients. This is the sort of thing that would usually be meant by 'thinking about the proposition that *p*'; just as 'thinking about Percy' means things like thinking that Percy is a foolish fellow, that he is possibly of noble birth, that he is liked by all the ladies. But do we really think about propositions *just as* we think about Percy? If propositions are logical constructions, no. The 'that' clauses which appear to have propositions as subjects can always be reworded in such a way that these ostensible subjects disappear; e.g. to think that the proposition that *p* is an absurd one is to think that it would be absurd to think (or say, etc.) that *p*; to think that it is possibly true is to think that it is possible that *p*; to think that it was believed by all the ancients is to think that all the ancients believed that *p*; and so on. To be thinking about a proposition is not to stand in a *relation* to it as one may stand to Percy in the relation of thinking him a foolish fellow, thinking him to be possibly of noble birth, liked by the ladies, etc. '— thinks that — is a foolish fellow' is a two-place predicate; its blanks keep places for names of objects. But '— thinks that the proposition that — is an absurd one', or '— thinks that it would be absurd to think that —', is not of this form; for here, exactly as in the more basic '— thinks that —', the second blank does not keep a place for a name but for a sentence.

It is the same with other thoughts that are ostensibly about *abstracta*. To think (falsely, of course) that 3 is greater than 4, is to think that, for any $\phi$ and $\psi$ (where these symbols are not name-variables but verb-variables), if exactly 3 things $\phi$ and exactly 4 things $\psi$, then more things $\phi$ than $\psi$. '3' here no longer even looks like a name of something; it is an inseparable part of the operator on verbs 'Exactly 3 things —', and we are not, in thinking this, *relating* ourselves to 3 as we might relate ourselves to Percy by thinking about him. Nor do we 'like fishing' in quite the same sense as we 'like Percy', though the senses are related. To 'like fishing' is to 'like to fish', and in 'X likes to $\phi$', '— likes to —' doesn't express a relation, i.e. isn't a two-place predicate, for its second gap is not for a name but for a verb. I suspect that the connection between 'liking' and 'liking to' is that to 'like Peter' is to like to see him, like to converse with him, and so on. The connection between thinking about Percy and thinking about a proposition is little more than that both boil down, though in different ways, to *thinking that* something or other, and that Percy's name, and the sentence expressing the proposition, occur as components of the sentence expressing the thought.

'About' is systematically ambiguous; what it means depends on what sort of name or quasi-name follows it. We say both 'thinking about Peter' and 'thinking about the proposition that $p$' because this is part of the whole game of 'nominalizing' what aren't really names of objects at all.

# 3

# PLATONISM AND QUANTIFICATION

1. *Syntactical versus metaphysical economy.* Russell's method, in his multiple relation theory of belief, of making propositions logical constructions, was seen to succeed in this only by forcing other abstract entities upon us in their place. Is not Ramsey's method open to a rather similar objection, namely that it rids us of an unpalatable type of abstract entity only by foisting upon us a new and equally unpalatable part of speech? Possibly; but before rejecting it on that ground we had better see what alternatives are actually open to us.

We cannot, in the first place, get rid of *all* distinctions of parts of speech. I doubt, for instance, whether we can entirely get rid of verbs, or of distinguishable uses of expressions which amount to using them as verbs. It is sometimes suggested that by drawing sufficiently freely upon abstract nouns we can explain what goes on when we use verbs. For example, it may be said that what I am doing when I say that Jones smokes is predicating smoking of Jones. But if the noun-verb form is supposed to require explanation, we still haven't got it if someone says 'When I say "Jones smokes" I predicate smoking of Jones, and in general when I say something of the form "$x\ \phi$'s" I predicate an attribute of an individual'. For 'I predicate an attribute of an individual' is itself of the form '$x\ \phi$'s', and if I do not understand this form when I encounter it in 'Jones smokes', how can I be expected to understand it when I encounter it in 'I predicate smoking of Jones'?[1] So we seem to need nouns and verbs anyway, and if we can equate sentences which appear to contain names of *abstracta* with ones from which these have disappeared in favour of the corresponding verbs, this is pure gain. If the statement 'When we say that Jones smokes we predicate an attribute of an individual' is *not* presented as an explanation but

---

[1] Cf. Wittgenstein [*Philosophical Investigations*, i. 134] and Frege [*Philosophical Writings*, pp. 54 f.].

as a simple generalization, it can indeed be given a good sense, and one moreover which doesn't entail the existence of *abstracta*; it then just amounts to 'When we say that Jones smokes, then for some $\phi$ and for some $x$ we say that $x$ $\phi$'s' (here we have only nouns, verbs, noun-variables, and verb-variables).

But can we do without connectives and adverbs? Perhaps we can, if we allow ourselves a sufficient battery of 'nominalizers'. If we have, for example, 'that' to form nouns (or noun clauses) out of sentences, we can say that 'If Peter comes John will stay away' means no more and no less than 'That-Peter-will-come implies that-John-will-stay-away', and that 'Peter will not come' means no more and no less than 'That-Peter-will-come is-false'. To deal with quantifications, we also need '-ing' to form nouns from verbs, and so, e.g. read 'Everything moves' as 'Moving is-universal'. We now have only nouns, sentences, $n$-place predicates for each $n$, and various 'nominalizers'. But if these are not to have further syntactical sub-divisions we must allow the attachment of *any* $n$ nouns to *any* $n$-place predicate, and must treat as meaningful, and as true or false, not only 'Moving is-universal' but equally 'Being-universal moves', 'Implying hates Peter', and so on. Not to mention 'Being-false-of-oneself is-false-of-itself' (which seems on the face of it to be true if and only if it is false); though it is only fair to say that there *are* ways of handling this one without inconsistency.[1]

The programme of Platonism, which eliminates parts of speech by multiplying entities, can certainly be carried through, and so can any number of compromises between its most thoroughgoing form and the opposite position advocated here. Most natural languages seem to enshrine such compromises. English, in particular, has plenty of connectives and adverbs as well as nouns and verbs of varying degrees of abstractness (it has, e.g. both the 'If . . . then . . .' and the 'implies' locutions), but the English speaker is a little uncomfortable both with 'Universality moves' and with 'For some $p$, $p$'. But the broad tendency of most natural languages is anti-Platonist; for even where abstract nouns and noun-clauses are freely introduced there is an admission that there is something fishy about them, since they are only allowed to go with their own kind of verbs— 'Colour implies extension' is all right, but 'Colour shaves exten-

---

[1] Cf. 'Entities' [*Australasian Journal of Philosophy*, Dec. 1954, 32. 3, 161–5].

sion' is not—and the allowable forms are in general those which can be plausibly equated to forms from which the abstract nouns and verbs have disappeared in favour of ordinary verbs and connectives. This in itself, however, proves nothing; usage can enshrine the folly or timidity as well as the wisdom of our ancestors; in the end we pay our money and take our choice.

2. *Bound variables as name variables.* Connected with the objection to introducing such curious parts of speech as that exemplified by '— believes that —', is an objection to quantifying variables that stand for sentences. This is said either to be illegitimate, or, if legitimate, to bring in 'propositions', as real abstract entities, by the back door. Its illegitimacy, or at least its being so out-landish as to be only resorted to in a desperation which our present problems do not warrant, has been particularly urged by L. J. Cohen.[1] It is quite unclear to me what his objections are, particularly since he himself quantifies predicate-variables without compunction. For sentences, as Peirce saw, are simply those $n$-place predicates for which $n = 0$; an $n$-place predicate is a sentence with $n$ gaps for names to go in, an 'open' sentence as it is now excellently called, and an ordinary or 'closed' sentence is one with no such gaps left. Cohen's use of quantifiers is thus one which slides easily down the $n$'s and then unexpectedly bumps to a stop at the lowest but one, leaving us gasping. It will be best, however, to examine Cohen's views (in Chapter 6) in their original context, that of formalizing certain paradoxes.

The objections of W. V. Quine[2] are more thoroughgoing, being objections to quantifications binding *any* variables but name-variables. When we employ a formula of the form 'For some $x$, $\phi x$', what it must always mean is 'There exists at least one thing such that that thing $\phi$'s', and what it presupposes is a set of objects such that the $\phi$-ing of any one of them would verify the quantified formula. These are the 'values' that the bound variable $x$ can take, and to be, in this sense, one of the values of a bound variable is, simply, to be an object, or to be. If we are prepared to write 'For some $\phi$, $\phi x$', the only possible way of reading this is to say that there exists at least one thing such that $x$ 'does' that thing; in fact it would be less misleading

---

[1] [*The Diversity of Meaning*, pp. 201–4.]
[2] [*From a Logical Point of View*, pp. 112 ff., etc.]

to use a single type-fount for all variables subject to quantification and not have predicate-variables but only the specific
predicate 'does', say '$D$', and rewrite the formula as 'For some $y$,
$Dxy$'. (Quine himself does not quite do this, but includes classes
of objects among the objects that constitute the values that his
variables take, and employs the specific predicate '$\in$', for 'is a
member of', giving us, e.g. 'For some $y$, $x \in y$'.) Similarly, if we
are prepared to write 'For some $p$, $p$', the only possible way of
reading this is to say that there is at least one thing such that
that thing is-the-case, and it would be less misleading to rewrite
the formula as, say, 'For some $x$, $Tx$'. To refer to particular
objects of which such things might be truly said, we need some
device like an initial 'that' for obtaining names from sentences
(cf. the 'nominalizers' required by the Platonists considered at
the beginning of this chapter), e.g. we might write '$\lambda p$' for 'that
$p$', and so form such sentences as '$T\lambda p$', perhaps with the law
that $T\lambda p$ if and only if $p$ (e.g. that-grass-is-green is-the-case if
and only if grass is green. This law might need some restriction
in order to avoid paradoxes). But we do not generalize from
this to 'For some $p$, $T\lambda p$', but to 'For some $x$, $Tx$', $\lambda p$ taking its
place among the objects which the bound variable $x$ can take
as values. Anything else that is real is also, of course, among
these objects. 'My tie is-the-case', for example, would be a
genuine sentence, and would serve to verify 'For some $x$, $Tx$'
if it were true; and its contradictory (which *is* true) does verify
'For some $x$, not $Tx$'. Though this seems nonsense enough, the
theory does draw a line between nonsense and sense quite sharply,
and does not attribute sense, for example, to 'My tie is-the-case if
and only if my tie'. For the law is not '$Tx$ if and only if $x$', which
would have as a special case '$T\lambda p$ if and only if $\lambda p$' ('That-grass-
is-green is-the-case if and only if that-grass-is-green'—equally ill
formed with the preceding), but '$T\lambda p$ if and only if $p$'. And even
the measure of nonsense which this procedure would involve
(like 'My tie is-the-case') is not nonsense which Quine himself
allows; it is, rather, the nonsense which he alleges to be involved
in binding sentential variables, or in coming as close to this as
his basic view of quantification would permit.

3. *Defence of non-nominal quantifications.* But why must we be
entangled in all this? The use of variables and quantifiers which

has been recommended in Chapter 2 seems to me straight-forward. If we start from an open sentence such as '$x$ is red-haired' and ask what the variable '$x$' stands for here, the answer depends on what we mean by 'stands for'. The variable may be said, in the first place, to stand for a name (or to keep a place for a name) in the sense that we obtain an ordinary closed sentence by replacing it by a name, i.e. by *any* genuine name of an individual object or person, say 'Peter'. The name 'Peter' itself 'stands for' a person, viz. the man Peter, in the sense of referring to or designating this man; and the variable '$x$' may be said, in a secondary sense, to 'stand for' individual objects or persons such as Peter. It 'stands for' any such object or person in the sense that it stands for (keeps a place for) any name that stands for (refers to) an object or person.

If we now consider the open sentence 'Peter $\phi$'s Paul', it is equally easy to say what '$\phi$' or '$\phi$'s' (the inflexion is purely idiomatic, with no logical significance) 'stands for' in the first sense—it keeps a place for any transitive verb, or any expression doing the job of a transitive verb, i.e. for any expression which forms a sentence from a pair of names. The question what it 'stands for' in the second sense, i.e. what would be designated by an expression of the sort for which it keeps a place, is sense-less, since the sort of expression for which it keeps a place is one which just hasn't the job of designating objects. Similarly with the two variables in 'If $p$ then $q$', or the one in 'James believes that $p$'. The variables here stand for, i.e. keep places for, sen-tences; but since it is not the job of sentences to designate objects, there is just no question what objects these variables 'stand for' in the second sense.

Turning now to sentences in which variables are bound by quantifiers, it will suffice to consider cases in which the quanti-fier is the particular or so-called existential one, 'For some —'. Consider, for instance, the sentence 'For some $x$, $x$ is red-haired'. The colloquial equivalent of this is 'Something is red-haired'. I do not think that any formal definition of 'something' is either necessary or possible, but certain observations can usefully be made about the truth-conditions of statements of this sort. 'Something is red-haired' is clearly true if any specification of it is true, meaning by a 'specification' of it any statement in which the indefinite 'something' is replaced by a specific name of an object or person, such as 'Peter', or by a demonstrative 'this' accompanied by an appropriate pointing gesture. In other words, 'Peter is red-haired, therefore something is red-haired' and 'This is red-haired, therefore something is red-haired' are good or valid inferences. The more formal 'For some $x$, $x$ is red-haired' is similarly entailed by any statement in which the quantifier 'for some $x$' is dropped and the remaining variable '$x$' replaced by some expression of the sort for which it stands, i.e. a name or demonstrative designating a particular object. I do not say that 'Something is red-haired' or 'For some $x$, $x$ is red-haired' is true *only* if there is some true sentence which specifies it, since its truth may be due to the red-hairedness of some object for which our language has no name or which no one is in a position to point to while saying '*This* is red-haired'. If we want to bring an 'only if' into it the best we can do, ultimately, is to say that 'For some $x$, $x$ is red-haired' is true if and only if there is some red-haired object or person, but this is only to say that it is true if and only if, for some $x$, $x$ is red-haired.

All this can be carried over, *mutatis mutandis*, into the discussion of quantifications over variables of other categories, and there isn't the least need to equate them with name-variables in order to see what is going on. 'For some $\phi$, Peter $\phi$'s' is true if any specification of it is true, meaning by a 'specification' of it any statement in which the indefinite verb 'does something' or 'acts somehow' is replaced by some specific verb or equivalent expression, e.g. 'is red-haired'; and it is of course true if *and only if*, for some $\phi$, Peter $\phi$'s. It hasn't any quite exact colloquial expression in English, because such variable verbs as 'do' tend to stand only for verbs of a particular sort—'Peter is red-haired' would not be thought of as a natural specification of 'Peter does something'. 'Peter is or does something' would perhaps catch the full generality of 'For some $\phi$, Peter $\phi$'s' well enough, and the way it works is clear.

'For some $p$, James believes that $p$' is similar. Its colloquial equivalent is, I suppose, 'James believes something' or 'There is something that James believes'. It is clearly true if any specification of it is, a 'specification' of it being a sentence in which the prefix 'for some $p$' is dropped, and the remaining variable $p$ replaced by an expression of the sort for which it stands, i.e. a sentence.

In all this I cannot see anything mysterious, or anything that need compel us to treat variables that do *not* stand for names of objects as if they did.

4. *Idiomatic higher-order quantification*. It is true, we may yet again admit, that forms like 'For some $p$, $p$' are not idiomatic English, perhaps even not idiomatic Indo-European, but it is not difficult to see the extensions of our ordinary verbal procedures which would yield equivalents of such forms. We form colloquial quantifiers, both nominal and non-nominal, from the words which introduce questions—the nominal 'whoever' from 'who', and the non-nominal 'however', 'somehow', 'wherever', and 'somewhere' from 'how' and 'where'. No grammarian would seriously regard 'somewhere' as anything but an adverb; 'somewhere', in 'I met him somewhere', functions as the adverbial phrase 'in Paris' does in 'I met him in Paris'. We could also say 'I met him in some place', and argue that people who use such locutions are 'ontologically committed' to the existence of places as well as ordinary objects; but we don't *have* to do it that way. Similarly, no grammarian would count 'somehow' as anything but an adverb, functioning in 'I hurt him somehow' exactly as the adverbial phrase 'by treading on his toe' does in 'I hurt him by treading on his toe'. Once again, we might also say 'I hurt him in some way', and argue that by so speaking we are 'ontologically committed' to the real existence of 'ways'; but once again, there is no *need* to do it this way, or to accept this suggestion. Questions to which the answer is a complete proposition are not, in English, introduced by a particular word, but are expressed by an inversion of word order ('Will he come?'); but we *describe* the asking of such questions by using the word 'whether' ('I asked whether he would come'), and in Latin the word *an* is used both to introduce and to describe a question of this sort. So we could simply *concoct* the quantifiers 'anywhether', 'everywhether', and 'somewhether', and translate, say, 'For any $p$, if $p$ then $p$' as 'If anywhether then thether'.[1]

What is in fact done in English, most often, is simply to extend the use of the 'thing' quantifiers in a perfectly well-understood way, as in 'He is something that I am not—kind', or in 'He

---

[1] Cf. A. N. Prior, 'Definitions, Rules and Axioms', *Proceedings of the Aristotelian Society*, 56 (1955–6).

believes something that I do not—that grass is green'. The first 'something' here is quite clearly adjectival rather than nominal in force, and I would contend that the sense of the second would be quite accurately represented by rewording it as 'He believes-that something which I do not—grass is green'. We also manage to express a variety of things by the word 'how' and its associated quantifiers. Wittgenstein said in his *Tractatus* that 'the general form of propositions is: This is *how* things are'[1] (italics mine), and in his *Investigations*[2] he has an illuminating comment on this, suggesting that in ordinary speech 'This is how things are' is employed as a 'propositional variable'. He gives as an example: 'He explained his position to me, said that this was how things were, and that therefore he needed an advance.' Here 'This is how things are' is given its sense by a previous whole sentence, just as a pronoun (the ordinary-speech equivalent of a name-variable) is given its reference by a previously occurring name. If we compare Wittgenstein's example with 'Jack bought some beans, and then he planted them', we might say that

$$\left.\begin{array}{c} \textit{Things are thus} \\ \text{is to} \\ \textit{I am in financial straits} \end{array}\right\} \text{as} \left\{\begin{array}{c} \textit{he} \\ \text{is to} \\ \textit{Jack} \end{array}\right.$$

And, more to our present purpose,

$$\left.\begin{array}{c} \textit{Things are thus} \\ \text{is to} \\ \textit{Things are some}\textit{how} \end{array}\right\} \text{as} \left\{\begin{array}{c} \textit{he} \\ \text{is to} \\ \text{some}\textit{one}. \end{array}\right.$$

'Things are thus' doesn't in itself tell you how things are, but 'Things are somehow' does, though it doesn't tell you much—only the logically true 'For some $p$, $p$'. This replaces a mere propositional form or function by an actual proposition, albeit a vague one, just as the mere propositional form or function '$x$ is coming' ('He is coming') may be replaced by the actual though vague proposition 'For some $x$, $x$ is coming' ('Someone is coming'). And 'However he says things are, thus they are' is a very natural rendering of 'For all $p$, if he says that $p$, then $p$'.

---

[1] Wittgenstein, *Tractatus Logico-Philosophicus*, 4.5.

[2] Wittgenstein, *Philosophical Investigations*, i. 134. (I have commented on this passage in my article on the 'Correspondence Theory of Truth' in the Crowell-Collier *Encyclopaedia of Philosophy*.)

Other question-words and relative pronouns may be similarly extended. I take the following from a Victorian popular work entitled *Enquire Within upon Everything* (London, 1869), item 168, 'Rules and Hints for Correct Speaking', example 35:

> *Here, there,* and *where,* originally denoting place, may now, by common consent, be used to denote other meanings; such as, '*There* I agree with you', '*Where* we differ', 'We find pain *where* we expected pleasure', '*Here* you mistake me'.

At least three of these four examples, and perhaps all four of them, involve 'propositional variables' in Wittgenstein's sense. 'There I agree with you' plainly = 'The $p$ such that you have just said that $p$, is such that I too would say that $p$'. 'Here you mistake me' = 'The $p$ such that you think that I believe that $p$, is such that I do not believe that $p$'. 'Where we differ' is a fragment; it might occur, e.g. in 'Where we differ, we keep silent in front of the children', i.e. 'For any $p$, if one of us believes that $p$ and the other not, neither of us says that $p$ or that not $p$ in front of the children'. The doubtful case is 'We find pain where we expected pleasure', but even this might well mean 'For some $p$, we expected to be pleased that $p$ but in the event were sorry that $p$'. These 'heres', 'wheres', and 'theres' are even a little suggestive of the 'logical space' of Wittgenstein's earlier work.

There is a suggestive little correction also in example 138 from the same place: 'Instead of "*This* much is certain", say "Thus much is certain", or, "So much is certain".' The suggestion would seem to be that what is 'certain' is not strictly speaking a 'this' but rather a 'thus and so' ('*how* things are'), though nowadays a non-nominal 'this', like a non-nominal 'something', would be considered fair enough.

5. *The ramified theory of types and Ramsey's answer to it.* Misgivings allied to Quine's are already to be found in the first edition of Whitehead and Russell's *Principia Mathematica*, where it is not quite held that non-nominal quantifiers are illegitimate, or that they are only ostensibly non-nominal, but it *is* held that such quantifiers must be treated with some squeamishness. But I do not wish to press this resemblance; I want to consider the *Principia* position at this point not because in itself it is *very*

relevant to Quine's, but because one of the first answers to it could also be turned into an answer to Quine.

The first edition of *Principia Mathematica* was marked by the adoption of what is now called the 'ramified' theory of types.[1] What is called by contrast the 'simple' theory of types is at bottom little more than a matter of being sensible about syntax. We need to distinguish between, e.g., predicates, which form sentences out of names, and higher-order 'functions' which form sentences out of predicates, and so on up this hierarchy. So if '$\phi$' is a verb, forming the sentence '$\phi x$', when attached to a name '$x$', it will not form one when attached to another verb—'$\phi\phi$', which might be exemplified in English by something like 'Smokes smokes', is just nonsense. This is straightforward enough. The 'ramification' comes in when within, say, expressions which form a sentence from a single name, we distinguish between ones which do and ones which do not involve quantifying expressions of the same sort. One of Russell's examples of the former is '— has all the qualities of a great general', i.e. 'For all $\phi$, if (for all $x$, if $x$ is a great general, then $\phi x$) then $\phi$ —', $\Pi\phi\Pi x C\psi x \phi x$'. A simpler example is '— has some quality or other', i.e. 'For some $\phi$, $\phi$ —', $\Sigma\phi\phi$'. Such a predicate, though in a sense of the same 'type', is said to be of a different 'order' from a simple '$\phi$' with no such internal quantifications of '$\phi$'s. According to the ramified theory of types, not only expressions of different types, but also expressions of different orders, ought to be represented by symbols of different sorts, and if we use '$\phi$', for example, for a 'predicative function of individuals', i.e. a one-place predicate with no internal quantifications over one-place predicates, we are not allowed to substitute *non*-predicative functions for '$\phi$' in theorems. For example, it is not legitimate to argue as follows: If there are no facts about a certain individual $x$, i.e. if for all $\phi$, not $\phi x$, then there is not *this* fact about $x$: that there are no facts about him; i.e. if it were true that there were no facts about $x$, it would be false; hence it cannot be true. Symbolically, we are proceeding in this argument as follows:

1. $C\Pi\phi N\phi x N\psi x$.

---

[1] The theory goes back at least to Russell's 1908 paper 'Mathematical Logic as Based on the Theory of Types', included in the collection *Logic and Knowledge* (1956), pp. 57–102.

'If for all $\phi$, not $\phi x$, then not $\psi x$' (where '$\psi$' can stand for any predicate at all)—this is ordinary quantification theory. Hence, by substituting $\Pi\phi N\phi$' for $\psi$', we have

2. $C\Pi\phi N\phi x N\Pi\phi N\phi x$.

Hence, by substitution and detachment from the *reductio ad absurdum* law $CCpNpNp$ (what implies its own falsehood is false), we infer

3. $N\Pi\phi N\phi x$.

The move from 1 to 2, according to the ramified theory of types, would involve an illegitimate substitution.

Similar distinctions must be made, according to this theory, within the 'type' of 'no-place predicates', or propositions. Hence the following well-known ancient argument cannot be carried through: If everything were false, one thing that would be false would be this: that everything is false. Hence it cannot be the case that everything is false. Or formally:

1. $C\Pi pNpNq$,

and so by substitution

2. $C\Pi pNpN\Pi pNp$,

and so by $CCpNpNp$,

3. $N\Pi pNp$.

This is blocked by the consideration that $\Pi pNp$ is not a proposition of the same 'order' as the '$p$' occurring within it, and so not of the same 'order' as the '$q$' which follows from it by instantiation from it, and so cannot be substituted for '$q$' to obtain 2 from 1.

Here propositions and predicates of higher 'order' are not absolutely ruled out, as by Quine, but they are treated as not being propositions and predicates in the same sense as those of lower 'orders'. The resulting restrictions on substitution turned out to exclude certain quite important forms of mathematical reasoning, and to save these Russell and Whitehead introduced a rather implausible 'axiom of reducibility', the details of which need not here concern us. In order to eliminate the necessity for this axiom, various logicians in the 1920s suggested 'simplifying' the theory of types by removing, for purposes of instantiating and substitution in theorems, the discrimination made between propositions and predicates of different 'orders', and dealing in other ways with the problems for which this discrimination was originally made.

One of the early advocates of this simplification was F. P. Ramsey, and one of his arguments in its favour began by taking over from Wittgenstein's *Tractatus* the view that universal and existential quantifications are simply very long conjunctions of the corresponding singular forms.[1] 'Something is red', for example, amounts to 'This is red or that is red or that other is red, etc., etc.'. 'For some $\phi$, $\phi x$', i.e. '$x$ is or does something', similarly amounts to '$x$ is red or $x$ is blue or $x$ smokes or $x$ drinks, etc., etc.'. And 'For some $p$, $p$' is similarly just 'Either grass is green or the sky is pink or $2+2 = 4$, etc., etc.'. All propositions, whatever their 'order', are simply truth-functions of singulars. To this, advocates of the ramified theory might reply that such conjunctions and disjuncts would not only have to be infinitely long but in the higher-order cases would have to include themselves as conjuncts or disjuncts, which seems impossible. For example, 'For some $p$, $p$' would have to be expanded to a disjunction in which one disjunct would be 'For some $p$, $p$'; this in turn would have to be similarly expanded, and so on. To this, Ramsey answered that not only is the difference between, say, 'For some $\phi$, $\phi x$' or 'For some $p$, $p$' and its disjunctive expansion merely a difference between the symbols used to express one and the same proposition, but also the difference between '$p$ and $p$' or '$p$ or $p$' and the plain '$p$' is merely a difference between the symbols used to express one and the same proposition; so that the *proposition expressed* does not have to 'contain itself' in the way that the objector alleges.

It is obviously easy to turn this sort of argument into a refutation of Quine's view that the introduction of higher-order quantifications brings with it new 'ontological commitments', i.e. commitments to a belief in the existence of new kinds of objects. For conjunctions and disjunctions of singulars, on any view, do not involve ontological commitments to any types of entity beyond those to which we are committed by the original conjuncts and disjuncts.

---

[1] F. P. Ramsey, 'The Foundations of Mathematics' (1925), included in the collection with the same title (1931).

This is a nice argument, but the assumption on which it rests is scarcely tenable. Ramsey himself ceased to believe that quantifications were just long conjunctions and disjunctions of singulars,[1] and arguments against it are well known; it is quite enough, it seems to me, to observe that to understand what is said by any of the supposed conjuncts or disjuncts it is necessary to know to which object the word 'this' refers, but nothing of this sort need be known to understand the quantified form. Nevertheless, something of the argument's force can perhaps be preserved even if this particular underlying error is abandoned. Quine would argue, I think, that the quantified forms $\Pi x \phi x$ and $\Sigma x \phi x$ do not commit us to the existence of any other *sorts* of entities than do the corresponding singular forms $\phi a$, $\phi b$, etc., which follow from the former and entail the latter. Why, then, should he suppose that the quantified forms $\Sigma \phi \phi a$, $\Sigma \phi \Sigma x \phi x$, etc., commit us to the existence of sorts of entities to which we are not committed by the forms $\phi a$, $\psi a$, $\Sigma x \phi x$ from which *they* follow? Or that the form $\Sigma p \delta p$ commits us to the existence of kinds of entities to which we are not committed by specific '$\delta q$'s from which *it* follows? The alleged emergence of these new ontological commitments has an almost magical air about it.[2]

6. *The symbolic necessity of abstracts.* Even, however, if Quine has provided no cogent reason for supposing that quantifying over non-nominal variables in effect nominalizes them, and commits us to a belief in abstract objects corresponding to them, there may *be* cogent reasons for supposing this all the same. And I want now to consider an argument of a rather technical sort that does seem at first to point to Quine's conclusion.

Logicians who believe in the real existence of, for example, 'properties', sometimes introduce names for them into their systems, or do what they describe as introducing names for them, by employing an 'abstraction' operator for forming such names from the corresponding predicates, or from 'open sentences'. Following Church, one may use for this purpose a prefix '$\lambda$', followed by a variable, followed by the open sentence in question. Thus if $\phi x$ is read as '$x$ is red', the property of

---

[1] *The Foundations of Mathematics*, pp. 237–8.
[2] Cf. C. Lejewski, 'The Problem of Ontological Commitment'.

redness would be symbolized by $\lambda x \phi x$. Again, if $A\phi x \psi x$ is read as '$x$ is red or $x$ is green', the property of being red or green would be symbolized by $\lambda x A\phi x \psi x$. To say that such a property *characterizes* an object $y$, we simply prefix its name to the name of the object, thus: $(\lambda x A\phi x \psi x)y$. Calculi which employ such abstraction-operators usually have a rule to the effect that an object $y$ has the property of $\phi$-ness if and only if $y\phi$'s, i.e. we may equate $(\lambda x A\phi x \psi x)y$ with $A\phi y\psi y$.

It might well appear that someone who does *not* believe in the real existence of properties just need not avail himself of any such notation. If, however, we consider ourselves free to employ quantifiers binding variables of any syntactical type that our systems contain, this piece of self-denial is not as easy to carry through as it may seem. Consider, for example, the following bit of higher-order universal instantiation:

(*a*)   $C\Pi\phi C\phi y\Sigma x\phi x CA\psi y\chi y\Sigma x A\psi x\chi x$,

i.e.

If (1) for all $\phi$, if $y\phi$'s then something $\phi$'s,
then (2) if $y$ either-$\psi$'s-or-$\chi$'s then something
either-$\psi$'s-or-$\chi$'s.

This is fairly straight sailing. But suppose we want to symbolize the more general principle of which (*a*) is a special case. We may first take it as far as we can by writing down

(*b*)   $C\Pi\phi\Theta\phi\Theta(\ )$

We want to put in the bracket something that will satisfactorily symbolize the alternation of a pair of verbs '$\psi$' and '$\chi$'. $A\psi\chi$ will not do, since $A$ has to be followed not by two verbs but by two sentences. However, we could introduce a new symbol '$A'$' which *does* form a verb from two verbs, by the definition

$(A'\phi\psi)x = A\phi x\psi x$,

turning the whole into

(*c*)   $C\Pi\phi\Theta\phi\Theta A'\psi\chi$

From this, by instantiation of '$\Theta$', we could get

(*d*)   $C\Pi\phi C\phi y\Sigma x\phi x CA'\psi\chi y\Sigma x A'\psi\chi x$,

and this, by the definition of '$A'$', would yield (*a*). This is in effect Leśniewski's solution to this type of problem. It is, however, a little *ad hoc*, and the λ-notation gives us a procedure which is generalizable. For (*c*) it gives us

(*e*)  $C\Pi\phi\Theta\phi\Theta(\lambda z A\psi z\chi z)$

which instantiates to

(*f*)  $C\Pi\phi C\phi y\Sigma x\phi x C(\lambda z A\psi z\chi z)y\Sigma x(\lambda z A\psi z\chi z)y,$

from which λ-conversion takes us to (*a*). It should be observed, moreover, that while λ-conversion will take us from (*f*) to (*a*), it will not take us from (*e*) to anything at all, since in (*e*) the λ-abstract is not attached to an individual variable. From certain contexts, in other words, 'abstracts' are not eliminable.

The Platonistic implications of the use of abstraction-operators, however, seem to me exaggerated. In the first place, the Lesniewskian variant $A'\psi\chi$ is quite clearly not an abstract noun at all but a complex verb; why should we say anything different about $\lambda x A\psi x\chi x$? It is, after all, used to form a sentence by being attached to a name; in fact, in the elementary case $(\lambda x\phi x)y$ it simply *replaces* the 'φ' in 'φy'. Expressions formed in this way are just wrongly described when they are said to be equivalent to abstract nouns, and to name properties. Such a description of these only becomes appropriate when they are allowed to *replace* name-variables, as would happen if we had such forms as $T(\lambda x\phi x)y$, to be read as '$\lambda x\phi x$ characterizes *y*', and supposed *Txy* to be well formed where '*x*' and '*y*' keep a place for any sort of names. We may, therefore, remain at ease about this variant of Quine's thesis.

It may be added that abstraction operators are *not* necessary in handling strictly *propositional* quantification. We not only have no difficulty with the instantiation 'If for all *p*, if *p* then *p*, then if (if *q* then *r*) then (if *q* then *r*)', $C\Pi p C p p C C q r C q r$, but we have none, either, with the more general 'If for all *p*, δ*p*, then δ*Cqr*', $C\delta p\delta p\delta Cqr$, where 'δ' is a variable for proposition-forming functors with one propositional argument. But quantification over *these* variables does make it necessary to introduce devices like λ-operators, to formulate laws like

$C\Pi\delta\delta\phi\delta\phi(\lambda p Cpp).$

7. *The syntactical ambiguity of quantification.* I must confess, however, that there is one feature of the logical syntax here being recommended which I do find a little embarrassing.

If we make names and sentences our basic syntactical categories, we can categorize $n$-place predicates, for example, as expressions which form sentences when attached to $n$ names, and which also (and in consequence) form $(n-m)$-place predicates when attached to $m$ names. Similarly, we categorize $n$-place connectives as expressions which form sentences when attached to $n$ sentences; and expressions like '— believes that —' fall into place as forming sentences from a name and a sentence. We can also have expressions forming a sentence when attached to a predicate, or to a name and a predicate, and so on. The general picture is reasonably clear. Where, however, do symbols like '$\Pi$' and '$\Sigma$', i.e. quantifiers in one sense of 'quantifiers', fit into this picture? It would appear that they form sentences when attached to a *variable* followed by a sentence. (The other sense of 'quantifier' is that in which the term means a symbol like '$\Pi$' or '$\Sigma$' *together with* the following variable.) But the syntactical category of a variable is generally taken to be the same as that of the corresponding constant. Hence, in systems in which quantifiers may bind variables in *any* syntactical category, their own category would seem to vary with that of the variables which they bind.

We might, alternatively, bring out the difficulty in the following way: Since, from the argument of the preceding section, it appears that at some levels we cannot dispense with devices like $\lambda$-operators, it would be sensible and economical to accept them from the start as the *only* operators which bind variables, and regard quantifiers as expressions which form sentences from 'abstracts'. Thus we rewrite $\Pi x C\phi x\psi x$, for example, as $\Pi(\lambda x C\phi x\psi x)$, and $\Sigma p Np$ as $\Sigma(\lambda p Np)$.[1] In the case of the simple $\Pi x\phi x$, i.e. $\Pi(\lambda x\phi x)$, the attached abstract is equivalent to the simple '$\phi$', so that we can also write this as $\Pi\phi$. This makes sense; the quantifier here functions as forming a sentence from a verb, as its ordinary-speech equivalent 'Everything' does. But we now encounter two problems, a lesser and a greater. The lesser problem is that of the syntactical category of the symbol '$\lambda$' itself, but perhaps all we need say about this is that '$\lambda$' is a symbolic dodge to get round a symbolic difficulty, and there's an end to it. But there remains the other problem: What is the category of '$\Pi$'

[1] This procedure is suggested in R. Feys [article in *Revue Philosophique de Louvain*, 44 (1946)], 74–103, 237–70.

and '$\Sigma$'? In $\Pi(\lambda x\phi x)$, i.e. $\Pi\phi$, the '$\Pi$' forms a sentence from a one-place predicate, and it does the same in $\Pi(\lambda x C\phi x\psi x)$, even if we don't in this case have a short equivalent. But in $\Sigma(\lambda p Np)$, 'Something is not the case', which we could also write as $\Sigma N$, the '$\Sigma$' forms a sentence from a one-place connective, or adverb.

# 4

## EXTENSIONALITY AND PROPOSITIONAL IDENTITY

1. *The fallacy of extensionalism.* 'To be a value of a bound variable is to be' is just a piece of unsupported dogma; and there is another such that gets in our way. Even where sentential variables are as freely bound by quantifiers as variables of any other sort, where connectives are admitted without question, and where the presence of both connectives and predicates makes it a simple matter to construct such mixed linking expressions as '— is green, and —', some resistance may be offered to putting '— believes that —' into this category. Basically the resistance is to putting 'X thinks that —' in the same category as 'it is not the case that —', i.e. to including both equally under 'one-place connectives'. This resistance comes from formal logicians who want to simplify their systems by saying that if the sentences S1 and S2 have the same truth-value then any compound sentences which differ only in one having S1 where the other has S2 must have the same truth-value also. If this 'law of extensionality' were true, and 'X thinks that grass is pink' and 'X thinks that grass is purple' were genuine compounds with 'Grass is pink' and 'Grass is purple' as components, then these compounds would have to have the same truth-value since the corresponding components do (both being false). It is, however, plain that a man may think that grass is pink without thinking that grass is purple. The moral drawn from this is that 'X thinks that grass is pink' is not a genuine compound with 'Grass is pink' as a component, or as it is technically put, not a genuine function with 'Grass is pink' as argument. But I cannot see the slightest reason, other than stubbornness, for not drawing the moral that the law of extensionality is false. There is, it is true, a large and interesting area of logical theory within which it holds, just as there is a large and interesting area of physical theory in which we can retain the laws of classical

mechanics; but I cannot see the least reason for claiming any more for it than that. I have been assured by some of its defenders that they can see immediately and intuitively that it is true; I can only say that such intuitions as I personally have about the matter are all to the contrary.

It is sometimes said, particularly by logicians of the schools of Leśniewski and Łukasiewicz, that if the law of extensionality is abandoned we must admit that some propositions are neither true nor false, i.e. that for some $p$, it neither is the case that $p$ nor is not the case that $p$. The argument for this is so riddled with confusions that it is painful to have to examine it; however, its proponents include logicians of such distinction that we had better go through with it. If all propositions are either true or false, it is argued, there can only be four propositional functions of one propositional argument—one, call it $Vp$ (for 'Verum $p$'), which is true as a whole whether its argument '$p$' is true or false; a second, call it $Fp$ (for 'Falsum $p$'), which is false as a whole whether '$p$' is true or false; one, call it $Np$ (for 'Not $p$'), which is true if '$p$' is false and false if '$p$' is true; and one, call it $Sp$ (sometimes read 'Assertum $p$', or 'It is the case that $p$'), which is true if '$p$' is true and false if '$p$' is false. And it is true of each of these functions that if '$p$' and '$q$' have the same truth-value then that function of '$p$' will have the same truth-value as that function of '$q$'. This can easily be verified in each case. $Vp$ and $Vq$, and $Fp$ and $Fq$, have the same truth-value (truth in the first case and falsehood in the second) whatever the truth-values of '$p$' and '$q$' may be. If '$p$' and '$q$' are both true, $Sp$ and $Sq$ will be both true, and $Np$ and $Nq$ both false; and if '$p$' and '$q$' are both false, $Sp$ and $Sq$ are both false, and $Np$ and $Nq$ are both true. So if any function does not obey the law of extensionality, it cannot be one of these four, and if there are other functions beside these, there must be more possible truth-values to generate them.

The very first step of this argument assumes what it claims to prove, namely that the only feature of '$p$' on which the truth-value of any function of it can depend is its own truth-value. For the list of possible functions simply does not include any which are, say, true with some true arguments and false with other true arguments. If 'X thinks that $p$', for example, were a function of '$p$', it would have precisely this character. Why on earth should not the truth-value of a function of '*p*' depend on some other feature of '*p*' than truth-value? To say that this is impossible is like saying that for any genuine function *fx* of a number *x*, whether *fx* is greater than 0 *must* depend on whether *x* is greater than 0—an assumption which is plainly false, for example, if the function is *x*—1; since in some cases when *x* is greater than 0, e.g. when *x* = 2, *x*—1 is also greater than 0, whereas in other such cases, e.g. when *x* = 1, *x*—1 is *not* greater than 0. Whether *this* function of *x* is greater than 0 clearly depends not on whether *x* itself is greater than 0, but on whether it is greater than 1. Similarly, whether it *is or is not the case* that X believes that *p* does not depend on whether *it is or is not the case* that *p*, but on whether *it is or is not believed by X* that *p*. Why on earth not?

2. *Frege on functions and values.* I suspect that the real villain of this piece is Gottlob Frege, and indeed that the rot set in with his invention of the term 'truth-value', in the mathematical setting which gave it its original meaning. Being greater than 0 is not, of course, strictly speaking, the 'value' of a numerical function for a given argument; its value for that argument is not a property of a number (such as being greater than 0), but a number. For example, the value of the function '*x*—1 for the argument 2 is 1, and for the argument 1 it is 0, and it has not a whole collection of values with a given argument in the way that with a given argument it has a whole collection of properties (when *x* = 2, for example, *x*—1 is greater than 0, less than 3, its own square, and so on). And Frege held that sentences designated or denoted objects called Truth and Falsehood in the same way that numerals, and formulas containing numerals, designate or denote numbers. Which number is denoted by a given numerical function-expression does depend on which number is denoted by its argument-expression (or expressions), and on nothing else. Hence, if the parallel holds, which out of Truth and Falsehood is denoted by a given sentential function must depend on which of them is denoted by its argument-sentence, and on nothing else. That it is not the case that grass is pink, we might say, not merely 'is true', in the way that 2—1 is greater than 0 (and also is other things, e.g. its own square), but *is Truth*, in the way that 2—1 *is the number* 1 (and is nothing

but the number 1). And that-it-is-not-the-case-that-grass-is-pink *is Truth* just because that-grass-is-pink *is Falsehood*, just as $(1+1)-1$ is the number 1 just because $1+1$ is the number 2. Equally, that-it-is-not-the-case-that-grass-is-purple *is Truth* just because that-grass-is-purple *is Falsehood*, just as $(3-1)-1$ is the number 1 just because $3-1$ is the number 2. And the 'Truth' which that-it-is-not-the-case-that-grass-is-pink 'is', is the very same 'Truth' which that-it-is-not-the-case-that-grass-is-purple 'is', just as the number 1 which $(1+1)-1$ 'is' is the very same number 1 which $(3-1)-1$ 'is'. There are not several Truths which different sentences might denote, any more than there are several number-1's denoted by such different expressions as '$(1+1)-1$' and '$(3-1)-1$'.

If Frege's parallel holds, all this follows. But of course it doesn't hold, and truth and falsehood are much more like properties (to be set alongside other properties) of what sentences denote, than themselves what sentences denote. They are not quite that, certainly; for sentences do not in fact denote anything, and propositions are things-with-properties only in a Pickwickian sense. But we know enough by now, all the same, to make this sense quite precise, and to use the things-with-properties locution harmlessly. For the matter of that, numbers are not things-with-properties (denoted by numerals) either, but here too we know enough now to use these locutions harmlessly —we know what we mean, e.g. if we say that 1 is greater than 0, viz. that for any $\phi$ and $\psi$, if exactly one thing $\phi$'s and nothing $\psi$'s, then more things $\phi$ than $\psi$. And there are innumerable things that we can 'say about propositions' in the sense in which we can say about them that they are true or that they are false, just as there are innumerable things that we can 'say about numbers' in the sense in which we can say about them that they are or that they are not greater than 0.

Frege himself knew that there was more to be said about the functioning of sentences than that they designate Truth or Falsehood, but said it so clumsily that it has been ignored or denied by those who have most eagerly taken up the other thesis. For he spoke of a 'sense' as well as a 'denotation' of sentences, and acknowledged that there were genuine functions of a sentence's sense as well as of its denotation; one such function of the sense of 'Grass is pink' being that expressed by the sentence 'X thinks that grass is pink'. But this is to make a dichotomy where there is none. When he thinks that grass is pink, what he thinks is precisely that whose not-being-the-case makes this thought a false one—it is certainly not true that there is one thing, the denotation of the sentence 'Grass is pink', which is not the case ('is Falsehood'), and quite another thing, the 'sense' of this sentence, which is believed by X. To have a false belief is to believe precisely what is not the case, not to believe something else which is merely connected in some obscure way with what is not the case. Truth-functions and belief-functions, in short, are functions of the same arguments; we must resist above all things the madness which insulates what we think from any possibility of directly clashing with what is so.

Frege's theory, to be fair, does not do quite that, and there would seem to be a possibility of constructing something like the ordinary theory (i.e. the one developed here) within this. For it would seem that the *Gedanken* or 'propositions' which constitute the sense of sentences do have, beside such properties as that of being thought by X, the property of being the sense of what denotes Truth or Falsehood (or, as Frege allowed in certain cases, neither) as the case may be; or, as Church puts it, they have the property of 'being a concept of' Truth or Falsehood (or, if we were to follow Frege here, neither). We thus have among the functions of Frege's *Gedanken* a set of functions related to one another in exactly the same ways as his functions of the True and the False are related to one another, and we can shear off these last as a superfluity. But the stone which we thus reject, the extensionalists have made the head of the corner.

Criticizing Frege is a thing one does 'more in sorrow than in anger', or in anger just because it is in sorrow; for there has perhaps been no greater philosophical logician, certainly none who has better appreciated the importance of carving up sentences in the right places if we are to see clearly what they are conveying—the technique of Chapter 2, though not its application, is wholly his.

Moreover, however misleading it may be to speak of sentences as denoting or designating truth-values in the sense in which proper names denote or designate individuals, it is not at all misleading, and is highly illuminating, to say that sentences have truth-values for their 'extension', in the way in which predicates have classes for theirs. It will be best to draw out this parallel after something has been said about propositional identity, but it may be noted now that part of the parallel consists in the fact that neither truth-values nor classes are genuine objects, both being 'logical constructions', and very similar logical constructions.

3. *Equivalence and propositional identity.* Pure extensionalism, i.e. extensionalism unmitigated by Frege's distinction between sense and denotation, in effect equates identity of what sentences mean with identity of their truth-value, i.e. with what is sometimes called their 'material equivalence'. For what extensionalists say about material equivalence, i.e. that all functions of materially equivalent sentences are materially equivalent, is really true of identity of meaning, or if we like to put it that way, of identity of the propositions which our sentences express. If the proposition that *p* really is the very same proposition as the proposition that *q*, then certainly any function of the proposition that *p* is the very same proposition as that function of the proposition that *q*. For example, if the proposition that *all bachelors are unmarried* really is the very same proposition as the proposition that *all unmarried men are unmarried*, then the proposition that *Jones wonders whether all bachelors are unmarried* is the very same proposition as the proposition that *Jones wonders whether all unmarried men are unmarried*.

This last contention may seem questionable—perhaps, even, almost as questionable as the law of extensionality itself—but before tackling that one, let us consider a more far-reaching objection to this way of talking, namely that once we start talking about propositional identity we are committed to abandoning the view that propositions are logical constructions, and to treating them as genuine objects. Identification, like quantification, may be said to involve an 'ontological commitment' to the straightforward objecthood of what is identified. But it is by no means clear that this is so.

Suppose we write *Ipq* for 'The proposition that *p* is the very same proposition as the proposition that *q*'. The apparent names 'The proposition that *p*' and 'The proposition that *q*' just do not occur in the complex *Ipq*, which only has the functor or operator *I* and the sentences '*p*' and '*q*', and in the verbal version these same apparent names can be considered as having no meaning or function outside the entire complex:

(1) 'The proposition that — is the very same proposition as the proposition that —'

(which is what we abbreviate to '*I* — —'), where the gaps are not for names but for sentences.

The form is exactly on a par with

(2) 'The proposition that — implies the proposition that —',

which is no more than a fluffed-up way of writing

(3) 'If — then —',

where these apparent names do not occur. The only difference is that we have no colloquial form analogous to (3) by which we can translate (1), but this is no more than an accident of language.

As to the *laws* of propositional identity, the fundamental ones are just *Ipp*, 'Every proposition is identical with itself', and the one already mentioned, that all functions of identical propositions are identical. If, using the symbolism of Łukasiewicz, we write *Cαβ* for 'If α then β', and use 'δ' as a variable standing for expressions which form a sentence out of a sentence, we may write this second law as *CIpqIδpδq*.

We are now in a position to examine objections to this law, and we begin with one hinted at earlier. It may well seem plausible to say that the proposition that all bachelors are unmarried is the very same proposition as the proposition that all unmarried men are unmarried, and yet that the proposition that Jones wonders whether all bachelors are unmarried is not the very same proposition as the proposition that Jones wonders whether all unmarried men are unmarried. We have the feeling that the second wondering would indicate much greater stupidity in Jones than the first wondering would. And precisely because there has been considerable argument among philosophers on this point, we are inclined to assent to the proposition that

(1) Many philosophers wonder whether the proposition that *Jones wonders whether all bachelors are unmarried* is the very same proposition as the proposition that *Jones wonders whether all unmarried men are unmarried.*

even though we are not at all inclined to assent to the proposition that

> (2) Many philosophers wonder whether the proposition that *Jones wonders whether all unmarried men are unmarried* is the very same proposition as the proposition that *Jones wonders whether all unmarried men are unmarried.*

But if the law $CIpqI\delta p\delta q$ is true, and if the proposition that all bachelors are unmarried is the very same proposition as the proposition that all unmarried men are unmarried, then the proposition that (1), which seems true, must be the very same proposition as the proposition that (2), which seems false. For (1) and (2) are just $\delta p$ and $\delta q$, with 'All bachelors are unmarried' for '$p$', 'All unmarried men are unmarried' for '$q$', and for '$\delta$' the functor

> Many philosophers wonder whether the proposition that Jones wonders whether —, is the very same proposition as the proposition that Jones wonders whether all unmarried men are unmarried.

There is here, I suspect, a confusion between wondering whether all bachelors are unmarried, and wondering whether what is expressed by the sentence 'All bachelors are unmarried' is true. And by 'wondering whether what is expressed by the sentence "All bachelors are unmarried" is true' I do *not* mean wondering, with respect to what is expressed by the sentence 'All bachelors are unmarried', whether it is true; for this is indeed the very same thing as wondering whether all bachelors are unmarried. What I mean by it is not this but wondering, with respect to the sentence 'All bachelors are unmarried', whether what it expresses is true. And a man might well wonder about this *without* wondering, with respect to the sentence 'All unmarried men are unmarried', whether what *it* expresses is true. For a man might very well not know that what the sentence 'All bachelors are unmarried' means is simply that all unmarried men are unmarried; and part of his reason for wondering whether what it expresses is true might be that he is wondering exactly what it is that it expresses. And in the case of our (1) and (2), this confusion may affect either or both of the outer and inner wonderings. That is, our wondering philosophers may really be wondering whether the proposition that Jones wonders whether what is expressed by the sentence 'All bachelors are unmarried' is true, is the very same proposition as the proposition that Jones wonders whether what is expressed by the sentence 'All unmarried men are unmarried' is true. Or again, they may be wondering whether the proposition expressed by the sentence 'Jones wonders whether all bachelors are unmarried' is the very same proposition as the proposition expressed by the sentence 'Jones wonders whether all unmarried men are unmarried', i.e. they may be wondering, with respect to these two sentences, whether they express the same proposition. There are other possibilities here also: but to go into them further would be tedious, and enough has been said to make our final answer clear. If there are *no* confusions of this sort, and if the person who is actually propounding the sentences (1) and (2) is himself using the sentence 'All bachelors are unmarried' simply to mean that all unmarried men are unmarried, and if this person is using the form 'X wonders whether *p*' to describe, not a wondering about a sentence, but a wondering what is the case—a wondering (in Jones's case) about the unmarriedness of bachelors, *i.e. of unmarried men*—then this person is *ipso facto* using (1) and (2) to mean the very same thing.

4. *The 'quotation-marks' objection.* There is, however, a much more substantial objection to the law *CIpqIδpδq*, if the variable 'δ' is taken to stand for *any* expression that forms a sentence from a sentence. For one way of forming a sentence from the sentence 'All bachelors are unmarried' is to put quotation-marks around it and prefix 'Jones utters the sentence' to the result; i.e. one expression which forms sentences from sentences is 'Jones uttered the sentence "— — — —"', where the inner quotation-marks are part of the sentence-forming expression I mean. The quotation-marks themselves, of course, do not form a sentence from the sentence inside them; rather, they form—if anything—the *name* of the sentence inside them; but the whole expression consisting of 'Jones uttered the sentence' plus the following quotation-marks, does seem to form a sentence from the quoted sentence. And it is quite clear that the proposition that Jones uttered the sentence 'All bachelors are unmarried' is *not* the very same proposition as the proposition that Jones uttered the sentence 'All unmarried men are unmarried'. It is even clearer that

the proposition that the second word in the sentence 'All bachelors are unmarried' is the word 'bachelors', is not the same proposition as the proposition that the second word in the sentence 'All unmarried men are unmarried' is the word 'bachelors'; though the sentence by which we have expressed the former proposition, and the sentence by which we have expressed the latter, are constructed by wrapping one and the same expression around the sentence 'All bachelors are married' in the one case and around the sentence 'All unmarried men are unmarried' in the other.[1]

These counter-examples are trivial and, one feels, sophistical, and yet they are difficult to exclude by any very clear rule or principle. It won't do to say, for example, that $CIpqI\delta p\delta q$ holds so long as the expression for which '$\delta$' stands isn't one that finishes up (i.e. 'finishes up' at the end or in the middle—wherever the argument-sentence is inserted) with quotation-marks. For (a) there are expressions which don't finish up thus for which the law just as obviously doesn't hold, and (b) there are expressions which do finish up thus for which the law fairly obviously does hold. For example—under (a)—'That all unmarried men are unmarried may be thus expressed to bring out its tautological character' surely does not express the same proposition as 'That all bachelors are unmarried may be thus expressed to bring out its tautological character' (cf. Quine's example in a different connection: 'Giorgione was so called because of his size'). Perhaps one could say there are 'implicit quotes' here—'thus expressed' means in the one case 'expressed by "All unmarried men are unmarried"', and in the other 'expressed by "All bachelors are unmarried"'. More importantly, there is, in 'thus expressed', a quite explicit reference to the form of words employed; the relevance of this will be indicated later.

As to the expressions which finish up with quotation-marks for which the law seems nevertheless to hold: (1) 'Jones said something with the sense of "All bachelors are unmarried"' might very well express the same proposition as (2) 'Jones said something with the sense of "All unmarried men are unmarried"', and quite certainly expresses a proposition with the same truth-value, if the quoted sentences do indeed have the

---

[1] I owe this objection to Professor C. Lejewski.

same sense or express the same proposition. It might be argued that (1) and (2) cannot express the same proposition because their translations into French are different, and are so regardless of whether or not French resembles English in being equally able to refer to unmarried men by one word ('bachelors') or by two ('unmarried men'). For, the argument runs, the French translation of (1) is 'Jones a dit quelque chose qui a le sens de "All bachelors are unmarried"', whereas that of (2) is 'Jones a dit quelque chose qui a le sens de "All unmarried men are unmarried"'. But this logicians' convention of not translating quoted expressions is by no means always followed in ordinary translation—it is proper enough when it is *quite* clear that we are only thinking of the quoted words *qua* sounds or marks (e.g. '"House" has five letters' must certainly be translated '"House" a cinq lettres' and not '"Maison" a cinq lettres'); but in e.g. translating a novel with a great deal of quoted conversation in it, it would be a poor translation which left all this in the original language.

In any case, there is something wrong in principle with the proviso we have suggested, depending as it does upon the presence or absence of a particular linguistic device, which might have had quite other uses, and which has a variety of uses even in ordinary English, and in other natural languages. The suggestion in fact involves a confusion between two very different ways of looking at such formulas as $CIpqC\delta p\delta q$. We may think of them, in the first place, as part of a rigorously formalized calculus; such a calculus will of course contain rules as to what we may substitute for the variable $\delta$ and still preserve theoremhood; but these permitted substitutions will not be expressions of ordinary English but expressions belonging to the calculus to which $CIpqC\delta p\delta q$ itself belongs. These expressions may or may note include devices which function as quotation-marks, or phrases ending with quotation-marks, sometimes do in English; if they do not, our difficulty doesn't arise; but of course if (in developing our calculus in detail) we deliberately see to it that they do not, we should be able to give reasons for such a course, and not just the reason that we would avoid trouble this way. The reasons must, in fact, be connected with the *other* way of looking at such a formula as $CIpqC\delta p\delta q$, to which we may now turn.

Even as part of a rigorously formalized calculus, the formula
*CIpqCδpδq*, like any other formula expressing a law of logic, may
be used to *say* something. Or perhaps more accurately, its
'closure', i.e. the result of binding all the variables in it by initial
universal quantifiers, may be used to say something: i.e. *this*:

(1) *ΠpΠqΠδCIpqCδpδq*,

or in semi-English,

(2) For all *p*, for all *q*, for all δ, if the proposition that *p* is
the very same proposition as the proposition that *q*,
then if δ*p* then δ*q*,

may be used to say something. And what these are used to say
in logic, is in general *not* something *about* sentences or expressions
at all. (2) may be partially instantiated, for instance, by

(3) For all *p*, for all *q*, if the proposition that *p* is the very
same proposition as the proposition that *q*, then if
someone brings it about that *p* then someone brings
it about that *q*.

And this in turn may be instantiated by

(4) If the proposition that all bachelors are fined £20 is
the very same proposition as the proposition that all
unmarried men are fined £20, then if someone brings
it about that all bachelors are fined £20, then someone
brings it about that all unmarried men are fined £20.

In (1), (2), and (3) it would in fact be natural to put an '*ipso
facto*' after the last 'then', e.g. to alter (4) to

(5) If the proposition that all bachelors are fined £20 is
the very same proposition as the proposition that all
unmarried men are fined £20, then if someone brings
it about that all bachelors are fined £20, then *ipso facto*
someone brings it about that all unmarried men are
fined £20.

Such an addition perhaps amounts to strengthening the second
*C* in (1) to an *I*, i.e. the proposition that (5) is perhaps the very
same proposition as the proposition that

(6) If the proposition that all bachelors are fined £20 is
the very same proposition as the proposition that all
unmarried men are fined £20, then the proposition

that someone brings it about that all bachelors are
fined £20 is the very same proposition as the proposition that someone brings it about that all unmarried
men are fined £20.

However this may be, it is important to notice that when we
pass from (2) and (3) to (4) the subordinate sentences which
finally replace $\delta p$ and $\delta q$ (in our example, 'Someone brings it
about that all bachelors are fined £20' and 'Someone brings it
about that all unmarried men are fined £20') are not *about* the
sentences which finally replace the '$p$' and '$q$' (in our example,
the sentences 'All bachelors are fined £20' and 'All unmarried
men are fined £20'), but they are about whatever these latter
sentences are about—in our example, the larger sentences, like
the smaller ones, are about bachelors, i.e. unmarried men, and
about what happens to such beings. (Indeed (4) in its entirety
is about bachelors, in the sense in which 'All bachelors are
bachelors' is about them.) And what is intended by (1) and (2)
is something that has *only* this sort of instantiation; we do not
count as instantiations (for what we mean by (1) and (2) is
something that does not *have* as instantiations) cases in which
the larger sentences are *not* about what the smaller sentences are
about, but are rather about these sentences themselves. Pseudo-
instantiations of the latter sort are excluded *whether or not* we are
using a language in which we sometimes talk about sentences
by first actually writing these sentences down (rather than spell-
ing them, Gödel-numbering them, etc.) and then surrounding
them with quotation-marks and their predicative appendages.

This position does not depend on any special view of *how*
quotation-marks contribute (when they *are* being used this way)
to talking about sentences themselves instead of about what the
sentences are about. In many circles the stock view is that the
quotation-marks plus the enclosed sentence constitute a *name* of
the sentence enclosed; but this may be and has been disputed.
Some would say that the quotations do not go with the enclosed
sentence but rather with what is on the *other* side of them to form
a peculiar sort of predicate, like ' "—" contains nineteen letters',
or 'John uttered the sentence "—" '. Some, again, would say
that the quotation-marks are *demonstratives* which *point* to their
interior, so that ' "The cat sat on the mat" has nineteen letters'

is rather like 'The cat sat on the mat. ← This has nineteen letters'. I incline to this view myself; and certainly if it is the correct view it is easy to classify the illusion involved in treating '"The cat sat on the mat" has nineteen letters' or '"The cat sat on the mat" was uttered by John' as compound sentences with 'The cat sat on the mat' as a component. This is simply the illusion of seeing two sentences as one, because they happen to stand in an interesting relation to one another.

One final word about this difficulty. Nothing could be more misleading and erroneous than to treat sentences containing (if that is the right word) other sentences in quotation-marks as a paradigm case to which the things that we are really interested in (thinking that, fearing that, bringing it about that) should be assimilated. It is a completely off-beat case which, having mentioned it, we are entirely justified in forgetting.

5. *Truth-values and classes.* We may now turn to the parallel between truth-values and classes which was hinted at earlier. To see this parallel accurately, something must first be said about what talk about classes really amounts to. The most elementary form of statement that is ostensibly about a class is a statement to the effect that something is a member of it, i.e. a statement of the form '$x$ is a $\phi$-er' or '$x$ is a member of the class of $\phi$-ers'. Such a statement is only ostensibly about a class, since it amounts to no more and no less than the simple statement '$x$ $\phi$s' (from which the appearance of being about a class as well as about $x$ has vanished). More complicated statements which are ostensibly about classes can all be defined in terms of this elementary form. For example, 'The class of $\phi$-ers is included in the class of $\psi$-ers' simply means 'Whatever is a member of the class of $\phi$-ers is a member of the class of $\psi$-ers', i.e. 'Whatever $\phi$'s $\psi$'s'.

But this is not the whole story. The complications come in when we wish to *count* classes. The notion of counting is bound up with that of identity. To say that exactly one individual $\phi$'s is to say that for some $x$, $x$ $\phi$'s, and for any $x$ and $y$, if $x$ $\phi$'s and $y$ $\phi$'s then $x$ is the same individual as $y$. To say that exactly two individuals $\phi$ is to say that for some $x$ and $y$, $x$ $\phi$'s, $y$ $\phi$'s, and $x$ is not the same individual as $y$, and for any $x$, $y$, and $z$, if $x$ $\phi$'s, $y$ $\phi$'s, and $z$ $\phi$'s, then either $x$ is the same individual as $y$, or $y$ as

$z$, or $z$ as $x$. The counting of propositions and properties involves higher-level quantifications and identifications of the same sort. 'Prior and Quine are agreed on exactly one thing', for example, could expand to

> For some $p$, both Prior and Quine believe that $p$, and for any $p$ and $q$, if both Prior and Quine believe that $p$, and both Prior and Quine believe that $q$, then the proposition that $p$ is the same proposition as the proposition that $q$,

where the last clause is understood as in the preceding section. And analogously to our understanding of that clause, we may understand the form

> The property of $\phi$-ing is the same property as the property of $\psi$-ing,

or more briefly

> To $\phi$ is the same thing as to $\psi$,

as constructed out of the verbs '$\phi$' and '$\psi$' by a two-place functor with one-place verb arguments, from the same syntactical box as the functor

> Whatever ( )s ( )s,

though it is not the same functor. The component 'The property of ( )ing' is not to be understood as forming a noun from the verb that goes into the gap, but as an inseparable part of the whole functor, so that the use of this form is not to be understood as committing one to the existence of properties any more than one is committed to this by the use of the form 'Whatever $\phi$'s $\psi$'s'. This being understood, 'There is exactly one property which applies to nothing' may be expanded to

> For some $\phi$, nothing $\phi$'s, and for any $\phi$ and $\psi$, if nothing $\phi$'s and nothing $\psi$'s, then to $\phi$ is the same thing as to $\psi$.

This is, of course, untrue; to be a mermaid, for example, is not the same thing as to be a centaur. On the other hand, the *class* of mermaids *is* the same class as the class of centaurs; there *is* exactly one 'empty class' or 'null class'.

This situation is sometimes misdescribed by saying that classes and properties are different entities. Misdescribed, because neither classes nor properties are entities at all. The real difference is that between the meaning of 'Exactly $n$ properties $\Phi$' and 'Exactly $n$ classes $\Psi$'. The former is defined in terms of quantification of verbs and verb-identity, while in the latter, verb-identity is replaced by common application, or what Russell calls 'formal equivalence'. To say that the properties of $\phi$-ing and of $\psi$-ing are 'formally equivalent' is simply to say that whatever $\phi$'s $\psi$'s and whatever $\psi$'s $\phi$'s. And to say that the class of $\phi$-ers is identical with the class of $\psi$-ers is simply to say that the properties of $\phi$-ing and of $\psi$-ing are formally equivalent. Hence to say that there is exactly one null class is to say that

> For some $\phi$, nothing $\phi$'s, and for any $\phi$ and $\psi$, if nothing $\phi$'s and nothing $\psi$'s, then whatever $\phi$'s $\psi$'s and whatever $\psi$'s $\phi$'s.

which is true. It is convenient to talk *as if* there were entities, classes, which are identical when their defining predicates apply to the same objects, but in fact to say that these entities are identical just *is* to say that the predicates apply to the same objects, and this in turn just *is* to say, of the given $\phi$ and $\psi$, that whatever $\phi$'s $\psi$'s and whatever $\psi$'s $\phi$'s.

Two-place predicates may be associated with 'relations in extension' in an exactly similar way. For example, to be both-father-and-mother-of is not the same as to be both-taller-and-shorter-than, but the corresponding 'relations in extension' *are* the same; for this is just to say that for any $x$ and $y$, if $x$ is both father and mother of $y$ then $x$ is both taller and shorter than $y$, and vice versa (the two implications being of course vacuously true, since no objects are related in either of these ways). Symbolically, identity of the class of $\phi$-ers with the class of $\psi$-ers is expressed by

(1)  $\Pi x E\phi x\psi x$,

and identity of the relations-in-extension corresponding to '$\phi$-ing' and '$\psi$-ing' by

(2)  $\Pi x\Pi y E\phi xy\psi xy$.

Similarly again, identity of the extensions of the three-place predicates '$\phi$' and '$\psi$' is expressed by

(3)  $\Pi x\Pi y\Pi z E\phi xyz\psi xyz$.

We can clearly go upwards from this as far as we like, but we can also go downwards from (1) one further. If '$\phi$' and '$\psi$' are '*no*-place predicates', i.e. complete propositions, we can say that their extensions are identical when we have

(o) $E\phi\psi$,

or in words 'If $\phi$ then $\psi$ and if $\psi$ then $\phi$'. This is the case when and only when either it both is the case that $\phi$ and is the case that $\psi$, or is not the case that $\phi$ and is not the case that $\psi$. So we concoct the term 'truth-value' for what we will describe as identical when condition (o) is met, just as we concoct the term 'class' for what we will describe as identical when condition (1) is met, and 'relation in extension' for what we will describe as identical when condition (2) is met. But we ought never to forget that these assumptions of identity mean no more and no less than the statement of the 'conditions' (o), (1), and (2).

The identity-conditions for 'numbers', it may be added, are analogous. 'For no $x$ does $x \phi$' is not the same function of $\phi$ as 'For all $x$, if $x \phi$'s then $x$ is not identical with $x$', but they apply to exactly the same $\phi$'s, i.e. we have

(4) For any $\phi$ (for no $x$, $x \phi$'s) if and only if (for all $x$, if $x \phi$'s then $x$ is not identical with $x$).

Hence, if we abridge 'For no $x$, $x \phi$'s' to '$ox\phi x$' and 'For all $x$, if $x \phi$'s then $x$ is not identical with $x$' to '$o'x\phi x$', we may say that o and o' are 'the same number'.

These odd uses of 'same', and inventions of entities for them to apply to, are of the utmost symbolic convenience, but failure to understand just what is going on when we avail ourselves of these devices has been philosophically disastrous. For example, it is fashionable to talk as if we have no right to speak of the identity of this or that unless we can formulate the 'conditions of identity' for the entities or quasi-entities in question. This demand is entirely in order when we are, as above, indulging in extensional abstraction, i.e. when what is involved is not *really* identity at all, and when it is therefore necessary to explain what surrogate for identity we are employing; but in most other cases the demand is a senseless one (identity, like quantification, just is what it is and not another thing). The error to which the present chapter is principally devoted—the treatment of truth-values as the *denotata* of sentences, and the confusion of propositional identity with material equivalence—is a special case of this more general muddle.

# 5

# THE OBJECTS OF COMMANDS AND QUESTIONS

1. *Propositions, commands, and questions.* The reasons which were originally given for believing that indicative sentences 'mean' or 'express' certain real but abstract objects called propositions, may be exactly paralleled by arguments for believing that imperative and interrogative sentences mean or express certain other real but abstract objects which we could call respectively 'objective commands' and 'objective questions'. Taking 'objective commands' first, it is clear that our issuing a command is one thing and the command that we issue another (for there may be different promulgations of the same command); and also that the imperative sentences by which we issue commands are different from the commands that we issue by them (for we may use different sentences, e.g. sentences of different languages, to issue the same commands); and again, what we command is obviously different from what our command is *about* (e.g. if we issue a command to shut a certain window, our command is about the window, but is not itself the window). So why not draw the conclusion that the furniture of the universe includes, besides commandings, imperative sentences, and objects like windows, certain further objects, of an abstract sort, which we may call 'objective commands'?

It is obvious, also, that this argument may be answered in the same way as the other. The things that we most often want to say about 'objective commands' are (*a*) that somebody issues them, i.e. that they are the objects of certain commandings, that they constitute *what is commanded* on such and such an occasion; (*b*) that they are or are not *binding* on us; and (*c*) that they are or are not *obeyed.* Let us put (*c*) on one side for the moment (as it obviously concerns the relation *between* imperatives and indicatives rather than a possible *parallel* between them), and concentrate on (a) and (b). As to (a), if we say that someone commands us, for example, to shut a certain door, we may remove the suggestion that this describes a relation between a person commanding and something commanded, simply by refusing to parse the whole as 'X commands us / to shut the door' (or 'X commands / the shutting of the door'), and parsing it rather as 'X commands us to / shut the door', where '— commands us to —' is not a two-place predicate expressing a relation between two named objects, but is rather an operator which forms a sentence out of a name on one side and an imperative sentence on the other. And as to (b), assertions that a command is or is not *binding* ostensibly divide objective commands into two groups analogous to facts and falsehoods; let us call them, for want of better names, 'norms' and 'impositions'. And, in the spirit of F. P. Ramsey on facts and falsehoods, we could say that 'The command to shut the door is a genuine norm' or 'is binding' is simply a long-winded way of saying 'Shut the door!' 'Endorsing' a command by saying that it is binding simply amounts to issuing the same command ourselves, just as 'endorsing' a proposition by saying that it is true amounts to asserting that same proposition. One might say that 'The command to shut the door is binding' looks like a statement about an entity called a command, just as 'The proposition that the sun is hot is true' looks like a statement about an entity called a proposition; we remove this suggestion in principle by rewording the former as 'You ought to / shut the door', just as we remove the other suggestion in principle by rewording to 'It is true that / the sun is hot'; and we finally simplify the former to 'Shut the door!', just as we simplify the latter to 'The sun is hot'. This final simplification is perhaps a more significant move in the imperative case since, although 'You ought to shut the door' no longer looks like an indicative sentence about the (objective) command to shut the door, it does still look like an indicative sentence, i.e. it looks as if 'You ought to —' constructed an indicative sentence out of an imperative one; but the equation of it to 'Shut the door!' (which is necessary if a Ramsey-type reduction is to be carried *right* through) shows that this appearance is illusory—'You ought to shut the door' is itself just a thinly disguised imperative (and 'The command to shut the door is binding' just a more thickly disguised one).

We did find, however, in handling the indicative cases, that the upshot of our discussion was not sceptical but was even in a sense 'realistic'; we could, at all events, give a good sense to such 'realistic' assertions as 'There are facts', 'There are falsehoods', 'There are facts which no one has ever asserted or ever will', and 'Such-and-such a proposition was true before anyone asserted it'. Can a good sense be similarly given to such statements as 'There are norms' (i.e. binding commands), 'There are impositions' (i.e. commands that are not binding), 'There are norms which no one has ever promulgated or will ever promulgate, but which are genuine norms all the same', 'Such and such a command was binding before anyone issued it'? If we could answer this question affirmatively, perhaps we shall be able to say that the view that ethical statements (like 'Stealing is wrong', or 'You ought not to steal') are disguised imperatives (like 'Don't steal'), is compatible with a belief in 'objective norms' (the 'absolute standards' of popular moral discourse). This would indeed be an important conclusion, but I shall suggest that it cannot in fact be drawn, and that the parallels between what can be done with indicative sentences and what can be done with imperative sentences break down at crucial points.

2. *Ramsey reductions yield no objectivity with commands.* As a formal symbolism, let us introduce the variables $\alpha, \beta, \gamma \ldots$ to stand for imperative sentences in the sense in which $p, q, r \ldots$ stand for indicative sentences, and use 'It is commanded to —' as an expression forming indicative sentences from imperative ones. Since 'There are facts' amounts to 'For some $p, p$', the analogous rendering of 'There are norms' (i.e. 'There are binding commands') would seem to be 'For some $\alpha, \alpha$'. So far as this is intelligible at all, this would seem to be not a statement but a command, namely the command 'Do something' in the most general possible sense—the sense in which even not doing anything would itself be a case of doing something. This extreme generality does not spoil the parallelism; quite similarly 'There are facts', or 'Something is true', is something that would be true even if nothing were true or a fact, for if it were really the case that nothing was a fact, *that* would be a fact (would be the case) and so something would be. This just means, of course, that it is *impossible* that there should be no facts. The command

to *do something* is similarly binding if any command at all is binding, even the command to do nothing; from which it follows that a command to do nothing (in this wide sense of 'do') *couldn't* be binding. But while the command to *do something* is a *necessary* command in the sense of being *a command that is binding if any command at all is binding*, it is for this very reason, and obviously, a *trivial* command, just as necessary truths, such as the truth that if it is raining it is raining, and the truth that there are truths, are in a sense trivial truths. But I doubt very much whether the people who want to maintain that there are 'absolute moral standards' would be satisfied with a *trivial command,* or indeed with any command, as an expression of their basic position.

When we try to give a similar account of 'There are impositions', i.e. commands that are *not* binding, we encounter new and special difficulties, and I shall therefore postpone consideration of this one, and look first at 'There are norms (binding commands) which never have been and never will be issued'. The indicative analogue, 'There are facts (true propositions) which never have been and never will be asserted', has for its Ramsey-style paraphrase 'For some $p$, $p$, though it never has been and never will be asserted that $p$'. The parallel paraphrase of the imperative analogue would therefore be 'For some $\alpha$, (do) $\alpha$, though it has never been and never will be commanded to $\alpha$', i.e. 'Do something which never has been and never will be commanded'. This is a command which has the logical peculiarity of being *unspecifiable*; there would be an internal inconsistency in an expansion of it to, let us say, 'Do something, for example turn your head to the right at 5 o'clock this afternoon, which never has been and never will be commanded'. But we have already seen that there is a like peculiarity about 'There are facts, e.g. the fact that $537+86251 = 86788$, which never have been and never will be asserted'; this doesn't make the unexpanded assertion false or even unplausible, and so perhaps the same peculiarity in the command just mentioned does not make it unbinding. But once again, this peculiar command seems quite remote from anything like an expression of belief in absolute moral standards.

As to such a statement as 'That the sun is hot was a true proposition (i.e. the sun was hot) before anyone said it was', the parallel to this in imperatives would be 'The command to shut the door was binding before anyone issued it', or 'You ought to have shut the door before anyone told you to', which by previous principles of translation would come out as something like 'Have-shut-the-door before anyone told you to shut it'; but a command to *have done* something, issued when the time for doing it has passed, would generally be regarded as unreasonable—reasonable commands always concern the future. But 'You ought to have shut the door before anyone told you to' doesn't *sound* as unreasonable as that, and in fact what is ordinarily meant by it is not 'You *now have* an obligation to *have shut* the door before anyone told you to' but rather 'You *had* (before anyone told you to) an obligation to *shut* it'. But how to introduce the past tense into an *imperative* form of speech in order to convey *this*, is completely obscure. That is not to say, however, that it cannot be done; it may just be that the symbolism so far introduced is inadequate. The trouble is clearly that the pastness is supposed to qualify the imperativeness of what is commanded, rather than its content; and our present symbolism does not bring out such distinctions.

3. *Reduction of objectivity of commands to objectivity of propositions.* We encounter a similar problem when we try to paraphrase 'There are impositions', i.e. commands (things commanded) that are *not* binding. It will be remembered that 'There are falsehoods' boils down, on Ramsey's analysis, to 'For some $p$, it is not the case that $p$'. But what is being generalized when we say 'For some $\alpha$, not $\alpha$'? What, in short, is meant by the negation of a command?—by, for example, 'Not (shut the door)'? Is this just the command not to shut the door, i.e. the command to refrain from shutting it (to leave it open)? But to issue this command is not equivalent to saying that the command to shut the door is not binding, is an imposition; it is equivalent, rather, to saying that the contrary command *is* binding, is *not* an imposition; and 'For some $\alpha$, not $\alpha$', in the sense of 'For some $\alpha$, do not $\alpha$', correspondingly is not the translation (on the principles we are trying to apply) of 'There are impositions' (i.e. non-binding commands), but rather of 'There are binding prohibitions' ('There are negative norms'). Once again, it is the imperativeness of the command rather than its content that we want to qualify, this time by denial.

We need, it would seem, something like Hare's 'neustics' and 'phrastics', but I see no valid reason why the latter should not be simply indicative sentences, as in the McKinsey–Hofstadter[1] symbolism which puts a 'shriek' or exclamation mark before a sentence '$p$' to construct, as '$!p$', the imperative 'Let it be the case that $p$' or (if the former sounds too much like a mere permission) 'See to it that $p$' or 'Bring it about that $p$'. Certainly one does not want the indicative component to be thought of as actually asserted in such contexts, but, as has often been pointed out, it isn't actually asserted in all indicative contexts either, e.g. when it is one member of a disjunction, or when it is preceded by 'It is not the case that'. We can then have '$!$not-$p$' for the command to see to it that $p$ *doesn't* occur, and 'not $(!p)$' for the mere 'You needn't bother', treated not as an assertion but as a permission to refrain. If the shriek can be thus modified by negation, it can perhaps also be modified by past-tense operators, to give such forms as 'Previously $!p$' for 'You ought to have seen to it that $p$'. These new forms are hardly commands (I mean verbal instruments of commandings) in the ordinary sense, but perhaps they could be all classified as 'imperatives' in a special technical sense. It could perhaps also be ruled that a single shriek is enough to make an entire complex, e.g. one like 'It is the case that $p$, and see to it that $q$', into an 'imperative', though one might add special operators like 'X issued the imperative to —' for forming indicatives out of imperatives (so that complexes in which all shrieks were immediately or remotely governed by such operators would *not* be imperatives).

This, however, is a rather radical alteration of our original programme. The variables we now have for binding are just the old propositional ones, and the formulas we are considering are going to look rather different. We are also going to be confronted with *choices* between formulas which we did not have before. It was, of course, a main motivation of the present change of symbolism to make distinctions which could not be made without it, but it gives us possibly more distinctions than we bargained for. For example, the command to 'do something' becomes either 'For some $p$, see to it that $p$' or 'See to it that (for some $p$, $p$)'. It is not at all obvious, if indeed it is true, that these two imperatives are equivalent. Neither of them, more-

---

[1] [ On the Logic of Imperatives', *Philosophy of Science*, 6 (1939), 446 ff.]

over, is now a simple parallel to the *assertion* 'For some $p$, $p$', i.e.
'There are facts', so that there is no longer much plausibility in
the identification of either of them with 'There are norms'. We
can still, if we wish, equate 'It ought to be the case that $p$' or
'You ought to see to it that $p$' with the simple 'See to it that $p$',
but we cannot find any secretly 'objectivized' or 'realized' drift
in this identification (there remains only the well-known and
much-exploited distinction between the imperative 'See to it
that $p$' and the psychological indicative 'It would please me
if $p$'). Indeed, the original crude arguments for 'objective commands' now seem misdirected; *what is commanded*, as distinct
from the act of commanding, is that a certain state of affairs be
brought about ('It is commanded that $p$'), and the objective
element here is just our old friend the Proposition; the distinction between commanding and asserting goes wholly into what
operates on this. If we want to be 'realists' in ethics, there
remains only the old way of introducing 'It ought to be the case
that —', or 'You ought to see to it that —' as an operator forming indicative sentences (which, if true, state *facts*) out of other
indicative sentences.

4. *Truth and obedience.* We do also, of course, still have a parallel
to *saying* truly or falsely, and to *believing* correctly or mistakenly,
in the obedience or disobedience that commands may meet
with, and the fulfilment or frustration that may attend wishes
and desires. To this topic, put aside a little earlier, we can now
briefly turn. 'X's command that it be brought about that $p$, has
been obeyed' does amount to 'X has commanded that it be
brought about that $p$, and it *has* been brought about that $p$',
just as 'X has truly asserted that it has been brought about that
$p$' amounts to 'X has asserted that it has been brought about
that $p$, and it *has* been'. Commanding, indeed, has certain pre-
suppositions that mere saying has not, with consequential limitations on what can be commanded. 'See to it that 2 and 2 are 4'
and 'See to it that the Battle of Hastings was fought nine cen-
turies ago' have a crazy quality about them which is absent
from the same sentences with 'It is the case that' in place of 'See
to it that'. But perhaps these peculiarities all derive from the
fact that a command is always a command to bring something
about, and one cannot bring about what is already the case, i.e.

it is the logic of bringing things about that has these special features, which are then transmitted to the logic of commanding. They are features which make it impossible to say that obedience to a command could consist, as what verifies an assertion could, in something that occurred or was done previously. We can, no doubt, say that what we wish for and ask for we sometimes already have (without realizing it) before we wish or ask for it, and it is certainly true that many things are the case and have been the case without ever having been wished for or demanded, but this is at least as far from an assertion of the objectivity of moral standards as anything else that we have been able to dig up in the theory of 'imperatives without indicatives of obligation'. Ethical objectivism without ethical facts remains the will-o'-the-wisp it always has been.

5. *Objective questions.* Turning now from imperatives to interrogatives: It is clear that the questions we ask may be distinguished from our asking them (the same questions may be asked on different occasions), and from the interrogative sentences that we use in asking them (different sentences may be used to ask the same question), and from the things that they are about; and this could suggest that over and above our questionings, our interrogative forms of words, and the particular things that we ask about, there are 'objective questions' or *interrogabilia.* And indeed a theory of objective *interrogabilia* is at least as plausible as a theory of objective *enuntiabilia* or propositions, and it seems perfectly sensible and true to say that there are questions that have never been asked and never will be. One of the earliest medieval logicians, Adam of Balsham, actually used the term *interrogabilia,* and thought that in a systematic presentation of logic we should examine *interrogabilia* first and *enuntiabilia* afterwards—a view of the priorities which is historically interesting, since Aristotle's classification of propositions in the *De Interpretatione* possibly began as an attempt to elucidate the affirmative and negative answers that might be given in the Greek questioning game of 'dialectic'. Adam of Balsham even had a proof that the set of *interrogabilia* can be put into one-one correspondence with a proper part of itself. In recent times, too, there has been some study of the formal properties of questions and of the question-and-answer relationship.

It is clear, too, that we *need* not be 'Platonists' about *inter-rogabilia*, and that we can avoid treating the parts of sentences which indicate *what is asked*, or what question some other sentence is an answer to, as if they were names. It is also clear, however, as in the case of imperatives, that nothing special, i.e. nothing beyond ordinary indicative sentences or sub-sentences, is needed to convey the objective 'content' of a question—the questioning attitudes can be put into the prefix. Harrah[1] has even suggested that a question simply *is* the indicative statement which is the disjunction of its possible answers, or in the case of some questions, the existential generalization of possible answers. For example, he identifies the question 'Is your tie red?' with the disjunction 'Either your tie is red or it is not', 'Is your tie red or is it blue?' with 'Either your tie is red or it is blue', and 'What colour is your tie?' with 'For some colour $\phi$, your tie is $\phi$'. There is no need to go this far; but we can certainly use expressions like 'Is it the case that . . .?' and 'For what $x$ is it the case that . . .?' to form questions from closed or open indicative sentences, and the prefixes that may form indicative sentences from closed or open indicative sentences include ones like 'He asked whether . . .', 'He wonders whether . . .', 'He knows whether . . .' and 'He asked (wonders, knows) for what $x$, . . .'. We can also give rules for finding equivalents for statements of the form 'He answered the question $Q$' and 'He knows $Q$', for different types of $Q$; e.g. 'He knows whether $2+2 = 4$' is equivalent to 'Either he knows that $2+2 = 4$ or he knows that $2+2 \neq 4$', and 'He knows what 2 and 2 are' to 'For some $x$, he knows that 2 and 2 are $x$'. (Note the distinction between this and 'He knows that (for some $x$, 2 and 2 are $x$)', which just means 'He knows that 2 and 2 are something', i.e. he knows that they have a sum.)

6. *Do we need question-variables?* There remain one or two small difficulties here, however. For example, 'For some $p$, no one has ever asked whether $p$' will not quite do as a rendering of 'There are questions that have never been asked', since there are other sorts of question besides 'whether' ones, and it is arbitrary to pick on that rendering rather than, say, 'For some $\phi$, it has

[1] [D. Harrah, 'The Logic of Question and Answers', *Philosophy of Science*, 28 (1961), 40–6.]

never been asked for what $x$ is it the case that $x$ $\phi$'s', or 'For some $x$, it has never been asked for what $\phi$ is it the case that $x$ $\phi$'s'. Must we say that in an accurate language we can have *simple* renderings only for the various distinct statements of the form 'There are *questions-of-the-kind-K* that have never been asked'? This seems awkward, and the only alternative seems to be to introduce special variables for interrogative sub-sentences (like 'whether $2+2 = 4$', 'what 2 and 2 are', etc.), and saying 'For some **p**, it has never been asked **p**'.

This proposal needs to be examined in some detail. It is clear that our language contains indicatives, interrogatives, and imperatives, and it seems a simple matter to use the prefixes 'Is it the case that . . .?' and 'See to it that . . .' to construct questions in the one case, and commands in the other, from given indicative sentences. In the former case, it can be from *any* indicative sentences, i.e. we can put 'Is it the case that . . .?' before *any* indicative sentence and thereby construct an intelligible question. With commands, it would seem that only a certain not very well-defined sub-class of indicative sentences is available for this treatment. ('See to it that $2+2 = 4$' and 'See to it that there was a glass on that table yesterday' have a nonsensical air about them). Also, our language contains means of stating that someone has *asked* a question or has *issued* a command. If we try to formalize assertions of this sort, keeping wholly to the object-language, we can either (*a*) first turn the indicative into a question or command, and then prefix some operator which forms *from* a question or command the indicative statement that the question has been asked or the command issued, or (*b*) attach directly to the original indicative an operator which forms a further indicative to the effect that what the original asserts has been questioned, or has been ordered to be brought about. In procedure (*a*), we start from '$p$' and then get, say, '$?p$' and '$!p$', and then get, say, $Q?p$ and $I!p$ (or $Imp!p$). Here the ordinary propositional '$p$'s and '$q$'s can stand for forms like $Q?p$ and $I!p$, but not for forms like '$?p$' and '$!p$', for which we would need special variables, say, '**p**', '**q**', '$\alpha$', '$\beta$', etc. In procedure (*b*) we go straight from '$p$' to say $Q\,p$ and $Ip$, which are here *parallel* to '$?p$' and '$!p$' but do not contain them. Ordinary English, it should be noted, doesn't *quite* do either of these things; it gets both questions and commands from indicatives by internal transformations (of 'The door will be shut', say, into 'Will the door be shut?' and 'Shut the door!'), and for the other job it uses slightly different internal transformations to get the required subordinate clause, e.g. from 'The door will be shut' we get 'He is asking *whether the door will be shut*', and 'He is asking *that the door be shut*'. At least, in the former case we *could* interpret what is done as procedure (*b*), with 'He is asking whether —' as the prefix that turns the simple indicative into the complex one; it is not quite procedure (*a*), though what happens in Latin could be interpreted either way (*an* is used equally to introduce an actual question or a clause saying what is questioned). We found reasons for regarding procedure (*b*) as quite good enough in the case of commands, but what is now being suggested is that for questions we adopt procedure (*a*).

It is important to notice that we are not suggesting that these 'question-clauses' are *names* of certain *interrogabilia* which people ask; i.e. although we parse 'He / asked / whether 2 and 2 were 4' in the way indicated by the lines, this does *not* mean that we are treating 'asked' as asserting that a *relation* held between one object, the questioner, and another object, the *interrogabile*. The second argument of 'asked', on this analysis, is not a name but an *interrogative sentence*. Nevertheless, this procedure gives rise to some grave problems. For it would seem that if 'whether *p*' and 'what *φ*'s' are distinct components when they follow 'He asked —', they are presumably also distinct sentence-components when they follow 'He knows —', for they don't seem to have a different sense in the two contexts. But then 'knows' would function on its own constructing a statement from a name and a question; whereas in 'He knows that *p*' we have insisted that the linking expression is not '— knows —' but '— knows that—'. Yet 'knows' doesn't seem to have different meanings in 'He knows what 2 and 2 are' and in 'He knows that 2 and 2 are 4', as it would have to if in the one case it had some sense on its own and in the other had no sense on its own, the unit being in this case 'knows that'. (If this way of putting the matter leans too heavily on a particular English idiom, we can restate the problem simply thus: If 'knows' in the one case forms an indicative sentence from an interrogative and in the other case from an indicative, it cannot be the same part of speech, let alone have the same meaning, in the two cases; yet it *seems* to have exactly the same meaning.)

A plausible solution to this set of dilemmas is to suggest that in 'He knows what $\phi$'s' and 'He knows whether $p$' there is something unstated but understood; what is meant is 'He knows *the answer* to the question whether $p$' ('the question what $\phi$'s'). We assume here a basic form built up from an indicative and an interrogative clause, namely 'That $p$ is the answer to the question **q**', where '$p$' stands for an indicative sentence and '**q**' for a question-clause like 'whether $p$' or 'for what $x$, $\phi x$'. 'He knows **q**' then expands to 'For some $p$, ($a$) he knows that $p$, and ($b$) that $p$ is the answer to the question **q**'. An adequate 'erotetic logic' will contain various theses about the question-and-answer relationship, e.g. 'For some $y$, that $y$ $\phi$'s is the answer to the question for what $x$, $x$ $\phi$'s', and 'Either the answer to the question whether $p$ is that $p$, or the answer to the question whether $p$ is that not $p$'. From laws of this sort, and the analysis of 'He knows **q**', we should be able to deduce our earlier equivalences, e.g. that of 'He knows what 2 and 2 are' to 'For some $x$, he knows that 2 and 2 are $x$'.

There still seems to be, all the same, a certain lack of simplicity and economy in the use of these interior questions and question-variables. No doubt there is a certain positive advantage in what we have called procedure ($a$), in that it exhibits the *relation* that undoubtedly exists between the forms 'He asked whether $p$' and 'Is it the case that $p$?', by making the latter a syntactical *part* of the former. A similar treatment of imperatives would have the same advantage. But the relation that we want to bring out here is surely a *semantic* one, that can be best brought out in the meta-language, e.g. by saying that for all $x$, if $x$ utters $\ulcorner ?p \urcorner$ then under normal circumstances he will be *asking whether $p$*, i.e. that is the purpose and sense of the form $\ulcorner ?p \urcorner$, and similarly with imperatives. So it still seems as if it would be best to use procedure ($b$) if we can.

What stopped us from using it in the first place, it will be recalled, was the fact that 'There are questions that haven't been asked' cannot be formally represented as 'For some $p$, it has never been asked whether $p$', because this form only covers a particular *type* of question; at least some of the questions that have never been asked are not of the form 'Is it the case that $p$?', but of such forms as 'For what $x$ is it the case that $x$ $\phi$s?' (e.g. 'Who has stolen my pencil?'). We want something that will cover questions of *all* forms, and 'whether' questions just don't seem to be reducible to 'what' ones. Perhaps, however, a reduction is possible the other way; perhaps 'Is it the case that $p$?' is reducible, say, to 'For what $\delta$, $\delta p$?', where the variable '$\delta$' is somehow confined to the operators 'It is the case that', and 'It is not the case that'. This, however, is at least awkward, and perhaps a further *philosophical* analysis of the process of questioning is needed before we can get the syntax of it straight.

7. *Objective questions as entailed facts.* At this point, it may be helpful to start from David Harrah's rather odd-sounding treatment of questions, mentioned earlier, in which each question is simply *identified* with a certain statement, namely the statement that we would normally say is *presupposed* by the question. To ask whether I am coming or going presupposes that I am doing one or other of these things, and so Harrah would say that the question 'Are you coming or are you going?' *is* the statement 'You are coming or going', and the question 'Whose hat are you wearing?' *is* the statement 'You are wearing someone's hat'. An *answer* to a question will then be a statement which *entails* the statement that the question *is*, but is not entailed by it; and a true or correct answer will be a *truth* which entails that statement, and is not entailed by it. Further specifications are also needed to make this quite right, but here we shall ignore them. The statement 'Jones is going', which answers the question 'Is Jones coming or going?' entails the statement which Harrah equates with this question, namely 'Jones is coming or going'. And the statement 'Jones is wearing Smith's hat', which answers the question 'Whose hat is Jones wearing?', entails the statement which Harrah equates with this question, namely 'Jones is wearing somebody's hat'. What I want to suggest now is that Harrah is, up to a point, right, and that a question *can* be regarded as a statement looked at in a certain way. And an *interrogabile* may be regarded as a *fact* looked at in a certain way. (This is not to say that there literally *are* either *interrogabilia* or facts; but since we know what to do with facts, we can begin to know what to do with *interrogabilia*, if we can make this identification.) Almost all facts (*all* facts except the totality of facts, if there is such a fact as that) are capable of being made in various ways more specific and determinate, i.e. all facts have facts which entail them without being entailed by them, e.g. the fact that I am sitting down

is less specific and determinate than, and is entailed by, the fact that I am sitting down on a chair; and this latter is in turn less specific and determinate than, and is entailed by, the fact that I am sitting on a chair belonging to U.C.L.A.; and so on. Facts may be said figuratively to *cry out for* further specification, though no more need be meant by this than that they are capable of it, and it is this which makes them questions, asked or unasked. Unasked questions are facts which are capable of being further specified, although no one has expressed a wish to know what more specific facts entail them; and in this sense *of course* there are unasked questions.

Possibly the notion of un-issued commands might be developed along analogous lines. A certain situation, we often say, *calls for* or requires a certain action or response, even if no *person* actually demands this action or response. Chisholm has recently discussed some of the formal properties of this selection of requirement.[1] But how far are we going to take this parallel? What I have called the entailment of one fact by another is a wholly 'objective' relation or quasi-relation between the facts in question; it holds, it is 'there', whether or not anyone makes use of it, e.g. to draw an inference, or to answer a question. It is just for this reason that it enables us to give a good sense to the statement that there are questions that never have been and never will be asked. If the notion of 'requirement' is to do the same job for unissued commands, it will have to have a similar objectivity, so that once again we have irreducible *moral facts*. If saying that a certain situation 'requires' a certain response merely expresses a wish that such a response should be forthcoming, the suggestion gives no more support to the idea of 'objective moral standards' than any of the others that we have considered.

[1] [R. M. Chisholm, The Ethics of Requirement', *American Philosophical Quarterly*, 1 (1964), 1–7.]

# 6

## A BUDGET OF PARADOXES

1. *The logic of falsehood, error, and insincerity.* Such forms as '*x* thinks that *p*', '*x* fears that *p*', '*x* says that *p*', may be said to express *propositional attitudes*. Their syntax—how they are formed from their components—seems so far reasonably clear, though we shall encounter some obscurities when we come, in Part II, to consider their 'objects' in the sense of what our fears, thoughts, assertions, etc., are *about*. But have they, beside this syntax, a logic? That is, are there special laws and rules associated with them? Numerous writers, such as J. Łoś, M. Fisher, E. E. Dawson, and especially K. J. J. Hintikka, have attempted to lay down such special laws and rules, but all the laws and rules proposed have a certain implausibility about them. For example, most of these writers lay it down that if *p* logically implies that *q*, and it is thought or asserted that *p*, then it must be thought or asserted that *q*. But nothing, unfortunately, is more common than for people to fail to draw the consequences of what they think and say. These writers are consequently driven to admit that what they are presenting is not really a logic of belief or assertion, but a logic of consistent or rational belief or assertion. And this is comparatively uninteresting; for what we would like to see is a logical and consistent handling even of man's illogicalities.

More promisingly, R. M. Chisholm has concentrated on the demarcation of propositional attitudes from other determinations of propositions (such as modal or truth-functional ones) by listing those laws which do *not* hold for them.[1] It is after all of some significance then when *p* logically implies that *q*, and *x* thinks that *p*, it does *not* follow that *x* thinks that *q*; this is itself something which can be expressed in a formula, and which has consequences that may be worth drawing.

---

[1] [See 'Intentionality' in *The Encyclopaedia of Philosophy* (ed. Edwards) and the bibliography thereto.]

It also turns out to be quite instructive—and it is on this that we shall concentrate here—to work out those logical features of propositional attitudes which are not peculiar to them but arise simply from features which they share with quite different determinations of propositions. They provide intriguing special cases of much more general logical laws. We shall consider a few examples of this in the rest of this chapter, some of them absurdly simple and commonplace, and some of them both complicated and scarcely credible (but there *are* surprises in logic).

Let us begin by laying down a few definitions. We shall presuppose the usual Łukasiewicz symbols for truth-functions and quantifiers, i.e.

$Np$ for 'Not $p$'

$Kpq$ for 'Both $p$ and $q$'

$Apq$ for 'Either $p$ or $q$'

$Cpq$ for 'If $p$ then $q$' (in the sense of 'Not both $p$ and not $q$')

$Epq$ for 'If and only if $p$ then $q$' (in the sense of 'If $p$ then $q$, and if $q$ then $p$')

$\Pi x$ for 'For all $x$' (and $\Pi p$ for 'For all $p$')

$\Sigma x$ for 'For some $x$' (and $\Sigma p$ for 'For some $p$'),

and take as undefined the functions $Bxp$, '$x$ believes that $p$', and $Sxp$, '$x$ says that $p$'. In terms of these we can define

$B(t)xp$, '$x$ believes correctly that $p$', as $KBxpp$, '$x$ believes that $p$, and $p$';

$B(f)xp$, '$x$ believes mistakenly that $p$', as $KBxpNp$, '$x$ believes that $p$, but not $p$';

$S(t)xp$, '$x$ says truly that $p$', as $KSxpp$, '$x$ says that $p$, and $p$';

$S(f)xp$, '$x$ says falsely that $p$', as $KSxpNp$, '$x$ says that $p$, but not $p$';

$S(s)xp$, '$x$ says sincerely that $p$', as $KSxpBxp$, i.e. '$x$ says that $p$, and $x$ believes that $p$';

$S(i)xp$, '$x$ says insincerely that $p$', as $KSxpNBxp$, i.e. '$x$ says that $p$, but does not believe that $p$';

$Ix$, '$x$ is insincere', as $\Sigma p S(i)xp$, '$x$ says something insincerely';

$Mx$, '$x$ is mistaken', as $\Sigma p B(f)xp$, '$x$ has some mistaken belief'.

There are other senses of 'insincere'; e.g. '$x$ says insincerely that $p$' might mean not merely that $x$ says that $p$ but does not believe it (this leaving open the possibility that he has not even thought about it or anyhow has no opinion about it either way), but that he says that *p* when definitely believing that it is not the case that *p*, *KSxpBxNp*. However, the above will do for our present exercise.

One theorem which is now easily provable is that whoever believes anything does so either correctly or mistakenly, *CBxpAB(t)xpB(f)xp*. For this just means that if a man believes anything either he does so and it is the case, or he does so and it is not the case,

    *CBxpAKBxppKBxpNp*.

This in turn is simply a special case of, and derivable by substitution from, the ordinary propositional-calculus thesis *CpAKpq KpNq*: If it is the case that *p*, then either it is the case that *p*-and-*q* or it is the case that *p*-but-not-*q*. Other substitutions in the same law give us *CSxpAS(t)xpS(f)xp*, 'Whoever says anything either says it truly or says it falsely', and *CSxpAS(s)xpS(i)xp*, 'Whoever says anything either says it sincerely or says it insincerely'.

The same apparatus can be used on the much discussed case of the man who says 'I do believe it's raining, but of course it really isn't'. There is obviously something badly wrong with this, but philosophers have found it remarkably difficult to say what it is. In the first place, there is nothing *inconsistent* in what this man says, and it could even quite easily be true. For what he is saying is *that he mistakenly believes that it is raining*, and this could quite easily be the case (people often *do* mistakenly believe that it is raining). But could he *mean it*? Could he be sincere? Could he *believe* that he believes mistakenly that it is raining? One's inclination is to say no, and to lay it down as at least one law of the logic of belief that *NBxB(f)xp*, i.e. *NBxKBxpNp* ('No one believes that he believes falsely that *p*'). This could even be proved, if we had as axioms

1. *CBxKpqKBxpBxq* (whoever believes a conjunction believes each of its parts).
2. *CBxBxpBxp* (whatever a man believes that he believes, he actually does believe).
3. *NKBxpBxNp* (no one both believes that *p* and believes that not *p*).

If a man believes that he believes falsely that $p$, i.e. that he believes-that-$p$-though-$p$-is-not-the-case, it will follow by 1 that he both believes that he believes that $p$ and believes that it is not the case that $p$. From this it will follow by 2 that he both believes that $p$ and believes that it is not the case that $p$. From this, and the proposition (our 3) that no one ever does both believe that $p$ and believe that it is not the case that $p$, it will follow that our initial hypothesis is false, i.e. that a man never does believe that he believes falsely that $p$. But of the three axioms here used, only 1 is at all plausible; 2 contradicts the fact that we often find, when it comes to the test, that we did not believe what we thought we did; and 3 contradicts the fact that men's beliefs are often inconsistent. (We shall find later that it is even *rational* to adopt a set of beliefs which cannot all be true, though one can hardly extend this to a mutually contradictory *pair* of them.) But even if it cannot be supported in this way, might not the proposition that a man cannot believe that he believes falsely that, e.g. it is raining, be self-evidently true? Perhaps it is, but we should not assent to it too hastily—human nature is odd enough for belief to take some curious twists, as with those who are afraid that God will punish them for not believing in his existence.

Let's leave it open, then, that the man who says that he believes falsely that $p$ *can* be sincere. Can he, then, say this without having *mistaken beliefs*? Surely he can; a man can say anything at all without having mistaken beliefs, for he need not believe what he says. It is sometimes argued that although a man's saying that $p$ does not *logically* imply that he believes it, it does 'imply' it in some other sense, or perhaps *he* 'implies', in saying that $p$, that he believes that $p$ (Moore). But I don't know what this means, unless it means either that people ought to be sincere, or that they usually are so, and we are therefore usually justified in assuming that they are. But in any case, even if a man does believe what he says when he makes the remark we are considering, it does not follow that this belief must be false, for as we have seen, what he says need not be false.

We are moving a little fast here, however. If a man believes what he says when he says that he believes mistakenly that it is raining, *this* belief (the belief that he believes mistakenly that it is raining) need not be mistaken; but if it is not, then another of his beliefs certainly is, namely his belief that it is raining. So

it does follow that if a man says that he mistakenly believes that
it is raining, then *either* he is insincere in what he says, *or* he is
mistaken—*either* in his belief that he mistakenly believes that it
is raining, *or* in his belief that it is raining. This proof is not
difficult to formalize. What is to be proved is that $CSxB(f)xp$
$AMxIx$, 'If $x$ says that he believes falsely that $p$, then either he
is mistaken (about something) or he is insincere (about something)'. With all defined expressions expanded by their definitions, it comes out as

$$CSxKBxpNpA\Sigma pKBxpNp\Sigma pKSxpNBxp,$$

'If $x$ says that $x$-believes-that-$p$-though-not-$p$, then either for
some $p$, $x$ believes that $p$ though not $p$, or for some $p$, $x$ says that
$p$ but does not believe it'. We can in fact prove this as a special
case of the more general

$$CfKgpNpA\Sigma pKgpNp\Sigma pKfpNgp,$$

where $fp$ and $gp$ may stand not only for $Sxp$ and $Bxp$ (which
when substituted give the preceding formula) but for any propositional functions of one argument whatsoever. Equating $A$ with
$CN$, the proof is as follows:[1]

$C(1)fKgpNp$
$C(2)N\Sigma pKgpNp$
$K(3)\Pi pNKgpNp$      $(2, N\Sigma p = \Pi pN)$
$K(4)\Pi pCgpp$      $(3, NKpNq = Cpq)$
$K(5)CgKgpNpKgpNp$      $(4, \text{U.I.})$
$K(6)NKgpNp$      $(3, \text{U.I.})$
$K(7)NgKgpNp$      $(5, 6, CCpqCNqNp)$
$(8)\Sigma pKfpNgp$      $(1, 7, CpCqKpq, \text{EG})$

There is thus no need to go outside ordinary truth and error,
and ordinary sincerity and insincerity—no need, in particular,
to appeal to such things as the social prerequisites of tolerable
conversation—in order to explain what is wrong with a man's
saying that he believes mistakenly that it is raining. What's
wrong with it is that whoever says this is either mistaken in what
he believes or insincere in what he says; and there is this wrong
with it whatever the reasons may be for valuing or expecting
correct belief or sincere utterance. And the proof that such an
assertion involves a man in one of these deficiencies uses nothing
but ordinary propositional calculus and quantification theory—

[1] [On this type of proof see Prior, *Formal Logic*, second edition, 319.]

we do not need to appeal to any principles belonging to a special logic of belief and assertion.

2. *The paradox of the preface.* A man is bound to be either insincere (in at least *something* that he says) or mistaken (in at least *something* that he believes) not only if he says that he mistakenly believes some specific thing, but also if he merely says that *some* belief of his is mistaken. And a man is bound to have said *something* false, not only if he says of some specific thing that he says it falsely, but even if he says, quite generally and vaguely, that *something* that he says is false. Similarly, *mutatis mutandis*, with beliefs. The point has been well developed by D. C. Makinson in what he calls 'the paradox of the preface'.[1] Authors have a habit of inserting into the prefaces of their books such remarks as 'All that is true in this work I owe to my wife, but all the errors are my own', and anyhow remarks to the effect that they are sure there are at least some errors in what they have written. But any man who says this, by that very fact makes it quite certain that there *is* at least one error in the totality of what he says. For either this remark is itself an error, or, if this remark is true, one of the *other* things that he says, and to which the remark refers, is erroneous. For the moment we may suppose that it *is* only to these other things that the remark refers. If we suppose it to refer to itself also, we shall be in far worse trouble, as we shall see; but even if we suppose it to refer only to the *rest* of the book, we are in trouble enough. For the man says in his book that *p*, and says in his book that *q*, and says in his book that *r*, etc., and he says in the preface, in effect, that either not *p* or not *q* or not *r*, etc.; and these together form an inconsistent set of assertions, in the sense that it is logically impossible that the whole set should be true. (Let a man assert just that *p*, that *q*, and that either-not-*p*-or-not-*q*, i.e. not-both-*p*-and-*q*; it is clear that he cannot be right all three times. Similarly with larger numbers.) And if all the remarks are sincerely made, including the one in the preface, the man is saddled not only with an inconsistent set of assertions but also with an inconsistent set of beliefs. The avoidance of such inconsistency is listed by Hintikka as one of the marks of 'rationality' in belief; but as Makinson points out, it may be very rational indeed (possibly a reasonable

---

[1] [*Analysis*, 25 (1964), 205-7.]

induction from what we have found with books we have written previously) to launch quite deliberately into the inconsistency just mentioned. No doubt the introduction of a quantitative element would ease the situation here; we may suppose it rational to believe things to the degree that they are likely, and it often happens that two things are each *more* likely than not, but their conjunction *less* likely than not, and it may happen that each of several things is more likely than not, though the conjunction of them all is downright impossible. It remains true, however, that Hintikka's equation of rationality with consistency is at this point implausible.

But let us now face the worst thing, and as it were transfer the assertion from the preface to the body of the book, and ask whether it will *now* be one of the truths that the man owes to his wife or just an error of his own. Let us, that is to say, include what the modest disclaimer of infallibility itself says among the things *of* which it says that at least one is not the case, and consider whether it is itself true or false. The answer seems at first easier than ever, for it can be rigorously proved, using only propositional calculus and quantification theory, that if X says in his book that something that he says in his book is false, then something that he says in his book *is* false, i.e. his statement is bound to be true. Writing '$\delta p$' for 'X says in his book that $p$', what he says in this case becomes $\Sigma p K \delta p N p$, and the theorem is

$$C \delta \Sigma p K \delta p N p \Sigma p K \delta p N p,$$

and the proof of this goes through whether '$\delta p$' stands for 'X says in his book that $p$' or for any other function of '$p$' whatever. Informally, but still quite rigorously, we may argue as follows: Let us try and suppose that the man's assertion (that something that he asserts in the book is not the case) is *not* true. Then there *will* be something said in the book which is not true. But that is just what this assertion says; so it must be true. The attempt to suppose it false thus destroys itself; true is the only thing it *can* be. Formally, we have

$C(1)\delta\Sigma p K \delta p N p$
$K(2)CN\Sigma p K \delta p N p K \delta \Sigma p K \delta p N p N \Sigma p K \delta p N p$    $(1, CpCqKpq)$
$K(3)CK\delta\Sigma p K \delta p N p N \Sigma p K \delta p N p \Sigma p K \delta p N p$    $(EG)$
$K(4)CN\Sigma p K \delta p N p \Sigma p K \delta p N p$    $(2, 3)$
  $(5)\Sigma p K \delta p N p$    $(4, CCNppp).$

But we seem to have this result too easily. For surely it is empirically possible, however unlikely, that the man's modesty in this assertion should be unwarranted, and that everything *else* he says in the book should be (for once) *true*. But if this crucial assertion itself cannot be false (as shown above), then *everything* in the book will be true, and the assertion (that *not* everything in the book is true) will be false after all. This last argument may be put in another way. We cannot assert in a book that something asserted in the book is not the case, unless something other than this both is asserted in the book and is not the case. No doubt in a book in which nothing else is asserted but truths, or indeed in which nothing else is asserted at all, anyone can inscribe, or have inscribed, the *sentence* 'Something asserted in this book is false', but he cannot then *say* by this inscription, or by any inscription, what would normally be said by this one, namely *that* something asserted in the book is not the case. He, or somebody else, could say this very thing elsewhere, and would then of course be saying it falsely, but he *cannot* (under those conditions) say it there.

Formally, we have to do here with the following sequence of theorems: First, we have already mentioned the theorem that if it is said in a certain book that something said in the book is false, then something said in the book *is* false, and quite generally

$$C\delta\Sigma p\overset{d}{K}pNp\Sigma pK\delta pNp. \tag{A}$$

From this we may easily deduce that if it is said in the book that something said in the book is false, then it is *truly* said in the book that something said in the book is false; and quite generally

$$C\delta\Sigma pK\delta pNpK\delta\Sigma pK\delta pNp\Sigma pK\delta pNp. \tag{B}$$

From this in turn it follows easily that if it is said in the book that something said in the book is false, then something said in the book is true, and quite generally

$$C\delta\Sigma pKdpNp\Sigma pK\delta pp. \tag{C}$$

From this and the first proposition above we easily infer that if it is said in the book that something said in the book is false, then something said in the book is false and something said in the book is true, and quite generally

$$C\delta\Sigma pK\delta pNpK\Sigma pK\delta pNp\Sigma pK\delta pp. \tag{D}$$

Here (B) follows immediately from (A) by $CCpqCpKpq$, (C) from (B) by $CCr\theta qCr\Sigma p\theta p$ (where $r = \delta\Sigma pK\delta pNp$, $q = \Sigma pK\delta pNp$, and $\theta' = K\delta$"), and (D) from (A) and (C) by $CCpqCCprCpKqr$. From this we may infer (with a little more difficulty) that if it is said in the book that something said in the book is false, then at least two distinct things are said in the book, and quite generally

$$C\delta\Sigma pK\delta pNp\Sigma(\geqslant 2)p\delta p, \tag{E}$$

where $\Sigma(\geqslant 2)p\delta p$, i.e. 'For at least 2 $p$'s, $\delta p$', is short for

$$\Sigma p\Sigma qKK\delta p\delta qNIpq,$$

i.e. 'For some $p$, for some $q$, both $\delta p$ and $\delta q$, and the proposition that $p$ is not the same proposition as the proposition that $q$'. We may also prove, again with a little more difficulty, that if it is said in the book that something said in the book is false, then something *other than that something said in the book is false* is said in the book and is false; and quite generally

$$C\delta\Sigma pK\delta pNp\Sigma pKNIp\Sigma pK\delta pNpK\delta pNp. \tag{F}$$

And from this we have, by contraposition, that if nothing except that something said in the book is false, is said in the book, then *that* isn't said in the book either; and quite generally

$$CN\Sigma pKNIp\Sigma pK\delta pNp\delta pN\delta\Sigma pK\delta pNp. \tag{G}$$

Formally, the proof of (E) runs thus:

$$
\begin{aligned}
&C(1)\delta\Sigma pK\delta pNp \\
&K(2)\Sigma pK\delta pNp && (1, (A)) \\
&K\Sigma qK(3)\delta q && (1, (A)) \\
&\quad K(4)Nq \\
&\qquad (5)NI\Sigma pK\delta pNpq && (2, 4, CpCNqNIpq) \\
&(6)\Sigma p\Sigma qKK\delta p\delta qNIpq && (1, 3, 5, \text{EG})
\end{aligned}
$$

(F) is almost proved by step (5) of the preceding, but we can set the proof out thus:

$$
\begin{aligned}
&C(1)\delta\Sigma pK\delta pNp \\
&K(2)\Sigma pK\delta pNp && (1, (A)) \\
&\Sigma pK(3)\delta p && (1, (A)) \\
&\quad K(4)Np \\
&\quad K(5)NIp\Sigma pK\delta pNp && (2, 4, CpCNqNIqp) \\
&\quad (6)KNIp\Sigma pK\delta pNpK\delta pNp && (5, 3, 4).
\end{aligned}
$$

And (G) comes from (F) by $CCpqCNqNp$.

*3. Some limits of self-reference.* This means that if we compose sentences in a language rich enough to be used for this type of self-reference, all kinds of apparently extraneous circumstances can deprive them, on particular occasions, of their normal meaning. But not only that; our little theorem does not have to be stated in terms of asserting—it is equally true, and similarly provable, that a man cannot *think* on a particular occasion, either correctly or mistakenly, that something that he thinks on that occasion is mistaken, unless he also thinks something *else* on that occasion which *is* mistaken; and he cannot *fear* on a particular occasion, either with justification or without, that some fear of his on that occasion is unjustified, unless he also has on that occasion some *other* fear which *is* unjustified. The fact is that not only the *truth* or the *justification* of what we say, think, or fear may depend on facts outside our assertions, thoughts, and fears—on any realist view, this is only to be expected—but the very possibility of *making* certain assertions, and the very possibility of *having* certain thoughts and fears, may depend on certain external things being or not being the case. In the case of assertions, we can blunt the edge of this by adverting to the distinction between our spoken or written sentences and what we say by them, but what corresponds to such sentences in the case of thoughts and fears? We may have the strongest impression that we can and do think and fear these things on occasions of the type mentioned; but to suppose that such impressions are correct is to suppose contradictions, to suppose that something both is and is not the case (e.g. that some fear that we have on a certain occasion both is and is not justified). This just cannot be. It is one of the uses of logic that it brings these hard truths home to us.

There is another side to this coin. If the man *does* make in his book some other assertion which is false, he then can make there the assertion which we have been discussing, and it will be (*a*) true, and (*b*) itself an 'assertion made in the book' in exactly the same sense as the false one is. Similarly, *mutatis mutandis*, with the thoughts and fears. We are *not* compelled to draw the conclusion, which a good many people *have* drawn, that a man can *never* make an assertion in a book about 'assertions in the book' in a sense which will cover that assertion itself, or have on a given occasion a thought (or fear) about 'the thoughts (or fears) which he has on that occasion' in a sense which will cover that thought (or fear) itself. To hold this would indeed preserve us from particular and casual deprivations of these possibilities, but only by depriving us of them all the time.

4. *Self-reference and particularization.* One piece of self-reference which, for all that pure logic can show, is perfectly legitimate, and which I think *is* perfectly legitimate, is one which some have found embedded in the Cartesian *Cogito*. Nobody can be mistaken in thinking that there is something he is thinking, for if he thinks that there is something he is thinking, then there *is* something he is thinking, namely that there is something he is thinking. The argument is a simple case of existential generalization. If I am thinking that $q$, then for some $p$, namely $q$, I am thinking that $p$ (symbolically, using '$d$' for 'I am thinking that —', $Cdq\Sigma pdp$). This holds good for any $q$ we like to take; e.g. my 'thinking that $q$' could be thinking that for some $p$, I am thinking that $p$. So we get by this substitution: If I am thinking that for some $p$, I am thinking that $p$, then for some $p$, I *am* thinking that $p$ ($Cd\Sigma pdp\Sigma pdp$).

It is sometimes said that this argument will not do because it involves us in an infinity of 'namely-riders'. The objection is that when we say 'Something $\phi$'s' this naturally means that for some specific thing, *that* thing $\phi$'s, so that it will always be possible in principle to expand it to 'Something $\phi$'s, namely so-and-so' (or 'Something $\phi$'s, namely, for example, so-and-so'). Since this expansion must *always* be possible where it is the case that something $\phi$'s, it can only be the case that there is something I am thinking if there is something, *namely so-and-so*, that I am thinking. Up to this point, the contention seems to me unanswerable. But it goes on: We cannot let this 'so-and-so' be merely 'that there is something I am thinking'; for it can only be the case that

(1) There is something, namely that there is something I am thinking, which I am thinking

if it is the case that

(2) There is something, namely that there is something (namely that there is something I am thinking) which I am thinking, which I am thinking.

And this in turn can only be the case if I can put a further 'namely so-and-so' after the new 'something' in the parentheses, so that if the only thing we ever put for our so-and-so is 'that there is something I am thinking' the ultimate specific backing which our original 'There is something I am thinking' requires will never be reached. In these further requirements, however, there is a fallacy.

Certainly if something $\phi$'s, then it must be that something in particular $\phi$'s—something must be true that is of the form '*This* thing $\phi$'s'. If something $\phi$'s, there must be some answer to the question '*What* thing $\phi$'s?' even if we do not know what it is. For example, it cannot be true *that I had something for breakfast*, unless some such specific thing as *that I had bacon for breakfast* is also true. (I cannot have had something for breakfast without there being some true answer to the question '*What* did you have for breakfast?'.) I *can*, however, *think that something $\phi$'s* without there being anything in particular *that I think $\phi$'s*—I can think that something $\phi$'s without there being any true answer to the question '*What* do you think $\phi$'s?' It can be true, for example, *that I think I had something for breakfast*, without any such specific thing as *that I think I had bacon for breakfast* being true (I can think that-I-had-something-for-breakfast without there being any true answer to the question '*What* do you think you had for breakfast?'—I may just think that I didn't miss the meal, without having any opinions as to what, in particular, I ate.)

Apply this, now, to the case in hand. If there is something that I am thinking, then there must be some specific thing which I am thinking, such as that two and two are four, or that grass is green, or that there is something I am thinking. (If there is something I am thinking, there must be some true answer to the question, '*What* am I thinking?') But if it is true that I think that there is something I am thinking, no such specific thing as that I think I am thinking that two and two are four, or that I think I am thinking that grass is green, or that I think I am thinking that there is something I am thinking, need be true at all. I can think that something $\phi$'s without having any thoughts as to *what* $\phi$'s, and this is true even if the '$\phi$'s' in question is 'is being thought by me'. It cannot be true, in other words, that there is something I am thinking, unless some such specific thing as the objector's (1) above is also true; but his (1) above *can* be true without any such thing as his (2) being true. At (1), the *necessary* 'namely-riders' finish.

In some cases, moreover, in which we think, and think truly, that something $\phi$'s, it may be in the nature of the case impossible that we should think, or at all events that we should think truly, anything more specific. For example, I may think, and in fact I do think, that there is something I have never thought of and never will, and this thought is a true one. But I cannot consistently think that I have never thought of some specific thing, say grass, and never will; for in this very thought I *do* think of grass or whatever it may be. (It was Berkeley's error to pass from the perception of the impossibility of this second thing, to a quite unwarranted denial of the possibility of the first.)

5. *The paradox of the truth-teller.* By the methods of section 2, we can show that no one can be thinking nothing but *that he is thinking something false*; contradictory consequences follow from supposing that he thinks nothing but this (in the sense of thinking this but thinking nothing else). On the other hand, it appears that there is nothing to prevent someone thinking nothing but *that he is thinking something*; we can even show that if he does think this, what he thinks is true. But what about the man who thinks nothing but *that he is thinking something true*, i.e. that for some *p*, he thinks that *p*, and *p*? Certainly it follows from his thinking this that he is thinking something; but it no longer follows that what he thinks is true. For what he thinks is not the mere *that he is thinking something*; that *is* true, on our supposition, but it is not quite what we are supposing him to think; what we are supposing him to think is that he is thinking something *true*. Whether what he *does* think *is* true depends on whether, for the *p* for which we have *dp* (that he thinks it) we also have the plain *p* (that it is the case). And since the only thing that he thinks is *that he thinks something true*, whether what he thinks is true depends on whether he does think something true, i.e. on itself. And this is indeed a vicious self-dependence, i.e. one which blocks the attachment of a 'namely-rider' that we *ought* to be able to attach. For we are trying to find out whether the man is thinking something that *is the case*, and it is not possible for 'something', or for 'something thought', to be the case without some *specific* thing, or some *specific* thing that is thought, being

the case. But the only specific thing that is relevant is the mere 'something' that we started with.

This reasoning is difficult to formalize. But its upshot would appear to be that if anyone is to think *truly* that he is thinking something true, there must be *something else* true that he is thinking (something more specific), and if anyone is to think *falsely* that he is thinking something true, there must be *something else* false that he is thinking (something more specific). From this, since if anyone thinks anything at all he must do so either truly or falsely, it follows that if he is to think at all that he is thinking something truly, there must be something else beside that (something more specific) that he is thinking. And more generally, it can never be that the only *d*-proposition (i.e. *p* such that *dp*) is the proposition that there are true *d*-propositions. That is, if the only *d*-proposition is the proposition that there are true *d*-propositions, then there are no *d*-propositions at all; or in symbols

$$C\Pi pCdpIp\Sigma pKdpp Ndq. \qquad\text{(H)}$$

Or transposing, if there are any *d*-propositions at all, then there is some *d*-proposition beside the proposition that there are true *d*-propositions:

$$Cdq\Sigma pKdpNIp\Sigma pKdpp. \qquad\text{(I)}$$

If we use *d*-subscripted propositional variables to stand for *d*-propositions only, (H) becomes

$$C\Pi p\ Ip_d\Sigma p_dp_dNdq_d. \qquad\text{(J)}$$

The first thing to be said about this formula, in any of its equivalent forms, is that it is *not* deducible from the simple basis earlier employed in deducing propositions (A) to (G). A simple proof of this is that that basis is consistent with the law of extensionality, according to which propositions which have the same truth-value are identical. That is, that basis would not lead to any contradiction if we read *I* as *E*. If, however, in (I) above we replace '*I*' by '*E*' and let *q* be *Cpp* and *dp* be *p*, we obtain

$$CCpp\Sigma pKpNEp\Sigma pKpp.$$

Detaching *Cpp* we have

$$\Sigma pKpNEp\Sigma pKpp$$

or

$$N\Pi pCpEp\Sigma pKpp.$$

However, the contradictory of this, $\Pi p C p E p \Sigma p K p p$, is easily provable, for example thus:

$\Pi p C(\mathrm{1}) p$

| | |
|---|---|
| $K(2) K p p$ | $(\mathrm{1},\ C p K p p)$ |
| $K(3) \Sigma p K p p$ | $(2,\ \mathrm{EG})$ |
| $(4) E p \Sigma p K p p$ | $(\mathrm{1},\ 3,\ C p C q E p q)$. |

Intuitively, since all true propositions are materially equivalent to one another, and if $p$ is true so is $Kpp$ and so therefore $\Sigma p K p p$, it follows that if $p$ is true it is materially equivalent to $\Sigma p K p p$. But from (I), with identity interpreted as material equivalence, it would follow that if anything at all were true (and $Cpp$, for example, *is* true), there would be a $p$ which was true but *not* equivalent to $\Sigma p K p p$. So it is clear that (I) is not deducible from any basis that is consistent with the interpretation of identity as material equivalence.

It is in fact not difficult to prove from (H) or (I) that there are at least two true propositions and at least two false ones.

6. *Cohen's treatment of self-reference, and of intentionality generally.* The second and more vexing version of the 'paradox of the preface' discussed in Section 2 is simply a variant of a modification made by P. T. Geach to the ancient paradox of the Cretan who says that everything said by a Cretan is false. (Geach observed that paradoxical consequences also follow from supposing a Cretan to say that *something* said by a Cretan is false.) On my view, the earlier paradox would of course be dealt with in a similar way. L. J. Cohen, however, as has already been mentioned, has objections to the binding of propositional variables, and to the treatment of belief as a function of which one of the immediate arguments is expressed not by a name but by a sentence. I have defended these procedures earlier, and will shortly offer criticisms of Cohen's alternatives to them, but his treatment of the paradox of the Cretan is instructive. I shall not reproduce it here, but will apply his methods to the second paradox of the preface, where they work equally well. I shall modify his verbalizations a little, but he himself suggests that these do not matter much; what is important for him is the syntax, which comes out most unambiguously in his symbolism.

Suppose we use

    $\phi x$ for '$x$ is (a sentence) in the book'
    $\psi x$ for '$x$ means that grass is green'
    $Tx$ for '$x$ is true'
    $p$ for 'Grass is green'.

Cohen would then represent 'It says in the book that grass is green' as

$$\Sigma x K K \phi x \psi x E T x p, \tag{A}$$

i.e. 'For some $x$, $x$ is in the book, $x$ means that grass is green, and $x$ is true if and only if grass is green'. If we now use $\phi x$ as before but $\psi x$ for '$x$ means that something in the book is false', the assertion that it says in the book that something in the book is false will come out as

$$\Sigma x K K \phi x \psi x E T x \Sigma x K \phi x N T x, \tag{B}$$

i.e. 'For some $x$, $x$ is in the book, $x$ means that something in the book is false, and $x$ is true if and only if for some $x$, $x$ is in the book and $x$ is not true'. My theorem (A) of Section 2, that if this is said in the book then something in the book *is* false will then come out as

$$C(B)\Sigma x K \phi x N T x \tag{C}$$

which ordinary quantification theory turns into

$$C \phi x C \psi x C E T x \Sigma y K \phi y N T y \Sigma y K \phi y N T y. \tag{D}$$

The proof of this, employing nothing but first-order predicate calculus, is as follows:

    $C(1)\phi x$
    $C(2)\psi x$
    $C(3)ETx\Sigma y K \phi y N Ty$
    $K(4)C\Sigma y K \phi y N Ty Tx$     $(3, CEpqCqp)$
    $K(5)\Pi y C K \phi y N Ty Tx$     $(4, CC\Sigma x \phi x p \Pi x C \phi x p)$
    $K(6)C K \phi x N Tx Tx$     $(5, C\Pi y \phi y \phi x)$
    $K(7)C\phi x C N Tx Tx$     $(6, CCKpqrCpCqr)$
    $K(8)C N Tx Tx$     $(7, 1)$
    $K(9)Tx$     $(8, CCpNpNp)$
    $(10)\Sigma y K \phi y N Ty$     $(9, 3, CpCEpqq).$

Our theorem (C) of Section 2, that if it says in the book that something in the book is false, then something in the book is *true*, goes into Cohenese as $C(B)\Sigma z K\phi z N Tz$, which has the same antecedent as the preceding, and is proved thus:

$C(1)\phi x$
$C(2)\psi x$
$C(3)ETx\Sigma y K\phi y N Ty$
$K(9)Tx$         (proved above)
$K(11)K\phi x Tx$     (1, 9, $CpCqKpq$)
$(12)\Sigma z K\phi z Tz$    (10, $C\phi x\Sigma z\phi z$).

We can also go on, using the ordinary theory of the identity of individuals, to prove theorem (E) of Section 2, that if (B) then at least two things are said in the book, i.e. for some $x$ and $y$, both $\phi x$ and $\phi y$, but not $Ixy$. Briefly, we have

$C(1)C(2)C(3)$
$\left.\begin{array}{l}K(10)\Sigma y K\phi y N Ty \\ K(12)\Sigma z K\phi z Tz\end{array}\right\}$     (proved above)
$\Sigma y\Sigma z K(13)KK\phi y\phi z KN Ty Tz$   (10, 12,
                                $C\Sigma y\phi y C\Sigma z\psi z\Sigma y\Sigma z K\phi y\psi z$)
       $K(14)CIyzCN Ty N Tz$   ($CIyzC\phi y\phi z$)
       $K(15)CIyzNKN Ty Tz$   (14, $CCpNqNKpq$)
         $(16)NIyz$                (13, 15).

What is interesting about this procedure is that as far as the theorems are concerned $x$ can be any sort of object and the $\phi$, $\psi$, and $T$ any sort of predicate, so that the formula (D) is equally exemplified by, for example, the statement that

> If John has a brown cow which is pregnant if and only if some animal of John's is not pregnant, then some animal of John's is not pregnant.

The proof is: *ex hypothesi*, if any animal of John's is not pregnant, the cow is; so if the cow is not pregnant, it is, so it *is* pregnant; and so (since this cow is pregnant if and only if some animal isn't) some animal of his isn't pregnant. We can then go on to prove (analogously with the other theorems) that some animal of John's *is* pregnant (since the cow is), and finally, that he must have at least two animals (since he has at least one which is pregnant and at least one which is not).

This transformation of the problem I find very appealing because it shows even more vividly than my own presentation of

it that nothing peculiar to the logic of belief is involved here.[1]
It is not difficult, however, to exhibit my own theorems, in their
original form, as special cases of something wider. For if we
replace Cohen's '$x$' by '$p$' and his '$\phi$', '$\psi$', and '$T$' by functions of propositions, we can prove (by steps exactly analogous
to those used above) the following variant of his (D):

$$C\delta pC\gamma pCE\xi p\Sigma qK\delta qN\xi q\Sigma qK\delta qN\xi q. \tag{E}$$

If in this we put $Cpp$ for $\gamma p$ and detach that antecedent, and
let $\xi p$ be the plain $p$ (i.e. let $\xi$ be 'It is the case that'), we obtain

$$C\delta pCE p\Sigma qK\delta qNq\Sigma qK\delta qNq.$$

If in this we put $\Sigma qK\delta qNq$ for $p$, we can detach the second
antecedent $E\Sigma qK\delta qNq\Sigma qK\delta qNq$ and obtain

$$C\delta\Sigma qK\delta qNq\Sigma qK\delta qNq, \tag{F}$$

which is just an alphabetic variant of our original theorem (A).
The upshot of this is that (a) I too can draw the parallel with
John's brown cow; and indeed my system brings out even more
than Cohen's the remoteness of the cases that can nevertheless
be brought together by the use of propositional calculus and
quantification theory, since even the syntactical construction of
(D) and (E) are different. Moreover, the fact that the '$\delta$' of (E)
constructs sentences from sentences whereas the '$\phi$' of (D) only
constructs sentences from names makes possible, in particular
cases, the simplification to (F) which has no parallel in Cohen's
system ($C\phi\Sigma xK\phi xNx\Sigma xK\phi xNx$ is simply ill formed—'$\phi$' cannot
take both sentences and names as arguments, nor can '$N$' take
names).

7. *Further defects in Cohen's treatment.* There are deeper defects in
Cohen's representation of the argument. Let us begin by
noticing that in the farmyard version of his theorems, it is not
in the least essential that the animal of John's which is pregnant
if and only if some animal of his is *not* pregnant, should be a
brown cow—the fact that it is one is not drawn upon at any
point in the proof. Similarly in the literary version no use is
made of the assumption $\psi x$, i.e. that $x$ means that something in
the book is false. For all the difference that it makes, that could

---

[1] Cf. Carroll's transformation of the Five Liars [*Symbolic Logic*, 4th ed., p. 192,
cf. pp. xiii–xiv].

be simply dropped—all the work is done by the other consti-
tuents. Or to put it another way, it would make no difference
to Cohen's theorem if the thing in the book *didn't* 'mean that
something in the book is false' but instead meant, say, that the
sky is blue; all that the argument requires is that the thing in
the book should be *true if and only if* something in the book is
false, and that is stated, not by $\psi x$, but by the other component
$ET x\Sigma y K\phi y NTy$. The complete mutual irrelevance of these two
components is what is strange here. It is just as strange in his
elementary form (A), $\Sigma x K K\phi x\psi x ET x p$, for 'It says in the book
that grass is green'. The intended expansion of this is 'For some
$x$, $x$ is in the book, $x$ means that grass is green, and $x$ is true if
and only if grass is green'; but the formula would obviously do
equally well for 'For some $x$, $x$ is in the book, $x$ *means that the sky
is blue*, and $x$ is true if and only if grass is green'. One wonders
why Cohen bothers to insert this component at all—why not
just render 'It says in the book that grass is green' as $\Sigma x K\phi x ET x p$,
'For some $x$, $x$ is in the book, and $x$ is true if and only if grass
is green'.

There is a reason for this complication, however. For 'if and
only if' is an 'extensional' function of propositions; '$p$ if and only
if $q$' is true so long as $p$ and $q$ are either both the case or both
not the case. It is, indeed, an essential part of Cohen's aim to
have none but extensional functions in his system. But because
of this extensionality, $\Sigma x K\phi x ET x p$ would be true if the only
thing said in the book meant, not that grass is green, but anything else that is the case, e.g. that the sky is blue. If the
only thing said in the book meant this, there *would* be an $x$ such
that $x$ is in the book and $x$ is true if and only if grass is green.
But it would be extremely odd to say, in this sense, that 'the book
says that grass is green'. Hence the extra component in Cohen's
translation of sentences of this form. It does no work in the
proofs in the last section; the reason for this comes out in a
different way in my own version of the paradox of the preface.
My theorems $(1)$–$(7)$ hold whatever functions of propositions
we put for the $\delta$ that occurs in them, extensional functions no
less than intensional ones. For example, if we let '$\delta$' be 'It is not
the case that —', or 'Grass is green and —', we will still have
$Cd\Sigma p K\delta p N p\Sigma p K\delta p N p$. For all that these theorems tell us, there
*might* be no functions of propositions but extensional ones.

# 7

## TARSKIAN AND NON-TARSKIAN
## SEMANTICS

PARADOXICAL and unparadoxical cases of self-reference form the subject of a vast and often entertaining literature; the later Schoolmen such as Buridan (cf. the eighth chapter of his *Sophismata*) were particularly ingenious in constructing examples. J. L. Mackie has recently done some useful classifying in this field (though he makes the case of the man who says that he thinks mistakenly that it is raining seem a little more mysterious than it really is).[1] But it is important to distinguish the problems discussed by both Mackie and myself—those discussed by myself at all events—from those discussed by contemporary writers on 'semantics', of whom the most important are Tarski and his school.

The notions of truth and falsehood which play a crucial part in the problems discussed in the preceding chapter, are *not* the notions of truth and falsehood analysed in Tarski's well-known paper.[2] The truth and falsehood with which Tarski is concerned are genuine properties of genuine objects, namely sentences. The truth and falsehood with which we have been concerned here might be described as properties not of sentences but of propositions; but this means that they are only quasi-properties of quasi-objects, and it might be less misleading to say that we have not been concerned with the adjectives 'true' and 'false' at all but rather with the adverbs 'truly' and 'falsely'. The basic form which Tarski defines is 'The sentence $S$ is a true one'; the form which we define is not this, but rather '$x$ says truly (thinks correctly, fears with justification) that $p$'. And we define this quite simply as '$x$ says (thinks, fears) that $p$; and it is the case that $p$', or more briefly '$x$ says (thinks, fears) that $p$; and $p$'. (Put 'It is not the case that $p$' for the second '$p$', or 'It is the

---

[1] ['Self-refutation: a Formal Analysis', *Philosophical Quarterly*, 14 (1964), 2–12.]
[2] [In *Logic, Semantics, Metamathematics*, pp. 152–278.]

case that $p$', and we have our definition of 'says falsely', or 'thinks mistakenly', or 'fears without justification'.) From these definitions and ordinary logic we may deduce all such statements as that

> (A)  If anyone says that snow is white, then he says so truly if and only if snow is white.

From Tarski's definitions and ordinary logic, we may deduce the truth of all such statements as

> (B)  The sentence 'Snow is white' is true if and only if snow is white,

and indeed for him the deducibility of all such statements is a criterion of satisfactoriness for a definition of truth. There may not seem to be that much difference between (A) and (B), but in fact the differences are considerable.

In the first place, there are quotation-marks in (B) but not in (A). These in fact belong to Tarski's informal exposition rather than his rigorous theory; but it is essential to his theory that in sentences of his type (B) the sentence which is *used* in the second clause should be *mentioned* (by name—however the name be formed) in the first. In (A), on the other hand, the sentence 'Snow is white', which is *used* more than once, is not *mentioned* at all (it nowhere goes into quotation-marks, or is spelt, or given a 'Gödel number', or named or designated in any way). (B) is *about* the sentence 'Snow is white', (A) is from beginning to end not about this but about snow.

The fact remains, however, that when we talk about people saying, thinking, and fearing certain things about what they say, think, or fear, this *sounds* as if it may involve forms of self-reference which a Tarskian semantics might show to be impossible; and the relations between what we have been doing and what the 'semanticists' are doing needs to be looked at more closely.

It is essential to Tarski's procedure to consider sentences as parts of a given *language*, and it is only as properties of sentences of a given language that 'truth' and 'falsehood' are defined by him. Moreover, the predicates 'is true' and 'is false' do not themselves belong to the language consisting of the sentences of which they are predicated. That is, if a sentence $S$ belongs to a certain language, the sentences 'The sentence $S$ is true' and 'The sentence $S$ is false' will not themselves belong to this language but to another, its metalanguage. The metalanguage must contain (*a*) some systematic method of *naming* the sentences of the given language, and (*b*) *translations* of every sentence of the given language (the simplest method of securing the second is for the given language to be a proper *part* of the metalanguage, so that its sentences are their own translations). The general type to which the sentence (B) above belongs is

 $x$ is true if and only if $p$,

where '$x$' represents the name, in the metalanguage, of that sentence of the given language of which '$p$' represents the translation.

In our own procedure, on the other hand, only a single language is used. The whole sentence (A) is a sentence of the language to which its component 'Snow is white' belongs. This gives rise to certain possibilities of self-reference which are not paralleled in Tarski's procedure. No sentence in any language considered by Tarski can discuss its own truth or falsehood, or the truth or falsehood of other sentences of its own language. But we have allowed it as possible—given favourable circumstances—for people to say, think, or fear things about the truth and falsehood of what they say, think, or fear; e.g. a man may—given favourable circumstances—say, think, or fear on some occasion that something that he says, thinks, or fears on that occasion is false, and this will itself count as one of the things that he says, thinks, or fears on that occasion. But this in itself constitutes at most a difference from, not a conflict with, what Tarski says. For we are not using 'true' and 'false' in his sense—Tarski and we are not discussing the same subject. (Or if Tarski does discuss languages in which this type of self-reference is possible, it is only to dismiss them as languages in which it is possible to prove self-contradictory sentences from commonplace logical and semantic premisses. But there is no conflict with any of our results in this.) We have roughly adumbrated a language which we can use to say certain things about what people say, think, and fear; but we have said nothing at all about the means, if any, which such a language might have for referring to its own sentences. At this point, such a language might very well, for all that we have said, have exactly the same limitations as the languages considered by Tarski.

It is necessary to distinguish at this point between the *negative results* and the *positive suggestions* of the preceding chapter. By 'negative results' I mean such things as that unless a man thinks *something else* on a given occasion, and something that is mistaken, he cannot even think on that occasion, let alone think correctly, that something that he thinks on that occasion is mistaken; or that a man cannot think mistakenly that there is something he is thinking. By 'positive suggestions' I mean such things as that, given favourable conditions, a man *can* think on a given occasion that something that he thinks on that occasion is mistaken; and a man *can* (on a given occasion) be thinking that there is something he is thinking, and be thinking nothing else but this.

As far as the negative results are concerned, they are not merely consistent with the results obtained by students of 'semantics', but the latter *could* be proved in exactly the same way. For what we have used in obtaining these results has been simply (*a*) ordinary propositional calculus, enriched with variables for expressions which form sentences from sentences, with quantifiers binding variables standing for sentences, and with an identity-function with sentences as arguments; (*b*) the ordinary theory of quantification applied to our special quantifiers; and (*c*) ordinary laws of identity applied to our special function. This is simply a fragment of the discipline which Leśniewski called prototethic, to which Tarski himself made important contributions in the early 1920s, and which is well known to be consistent. Tarski defines truth in the Ramseyan sense as well as in his own. The full theory of prototethic also contains the law of extensionality, which we have not used and in fact deny; but Tarski, although he appears inclined to accept it, has himself proved its independence of the theory that we *have* used.[1] Neither, however, have we used the *denial* of the law of extensionality in proving the theorems mentioned above, i.e. we have proved nothing inconsistent with this law.

Our fragment of prototethic could, in fact, quite easily have formed the logical portion of a Tarskian metalanguage; and had it done so, one possible substitution for our variable '$\delta$'

---

[1] [*Logic, Semantics, Metamathematics*, p. 8.]

would have been 'The sentence $S$ (of the sub-language) is true if and only if —'. This would turn, for example, our theorem

$$C\delta\Sigma pK\delta pNp\Sigma pK\delta pNp$$

into

> 'If the sentence $S$ is true if and only if for some $p$, both ($S$ is true if and only if $p$) and (not $p$), then for some $p$, both ($S$ is true if and only if $p$) and (not $p$)',

i.e.

> 'If the sentence $S$ is true if and only if for some *false* $p$, $S$ is true if and only if $p$, then for some false $p$, $S$ is true if and only if $p$.'

This is a Tarskian theorem in any case, since it is an implication with an antecedent which is provably false. For the antecedent has the form '$q$ if and only if (for some false $p$, $q$ if and only if $p$)'. But 'For some false $p$, $q$ if and only if $p$' is equivalent to 'Not $q$'; so the antecedent is equivalent to '$q$ if and only if not $q$', which is a contradiction. That is to say, *no* sentence $S$ is true if and only if for some false $p$, $S$ is true if and only if $p$.

Our theorem, however, also covers substitutions for '$\delta$' which *don't* turn its antecedent into something necessarily false. One such substitution, we have contended, is '$x$ says (thinks, fears) on such-and-such an occasion that', i.e. we have suggested that on some occasions, $x$ may succeed in saying (thinking, fearing) on this occasion that something that $x$ says (thinks, fears) on this occasion is false. This, of course, is not a 'negative result' but a 'positive suggestion'. But even if we confine our substitutions for '$\delta$' to functions available in an extensional logic, $\delta\Sigma pK\delta pNp$ isn't always false; for example, if we let '$\delta$' be 'It either is or is not the case that —', *anything* beginning with this '$\delta$' (including $\delta\Sigma pK\delta pNp$) is bound to be true; and for this '$\delta$', the consequent of our theorem, $\Sigma pK\delta pNp$, is also bound to be true, for there *is* a $p$, namely any $p$ that is false, for which we have both 'It either is or is not the case that $p$' and 'It is not the case that $p$'.

In the preceding chapter, however, I have *not* used this fragment of protothetic as part of a Tarskian metalanguage, that is I have not extended it by introducing expressions like '$S$ is a true sentence if and only if —', or expressions in terms of which this one might be defined. Rather, I have extended it by introducing expressions of the general type of 'x says that —', or 'x says on such and such an occasion that —', or 'x says during the interval t–t' that —'. If we abridge the last expression to 'Sx', 'Sxp' will now be formally available for substitution in such theorems as *CSxΣpKSxpNpΣpKSxpNp*. I have pointed out, and indeed proved, that, whatever language a person x may use to say things, he cannot say between t and t' that something that he says between t and t' is false unless he says something else between t and t'; so that if he enunciates any sentence between t and t', even one which he would normally use to say that something that he says between t and t' is false, he cannot in fact say *this* by it if he does nothing else that could be called 'saying' something during that interval—which of course could very well happen. I have recorded this result in a detached way as one of the misfortunes that may befall the sentences used by poor old x; but in fact what sentences could be more suitable for x to use on one of these occasions than those of the very language that I have devised to formulate my theorems? In fact, as a user and recommender of this language, am not *I* in as much danger as anyone could be of falling into x's predicament?

Let x be Prior, in fact. With 'x' thus understood, I can surely formulate the theorem just mentioned, *CSxΣpKSxpNpΣpKSxpNp*. But I could hardly formulate this theorem if I could not formulate its consequent *ΣpKSxpNp*. And I have assumed that if I read off or inscribe this formula *ΣpKSxpNp*, I thereby say that something that Prior says between t and t' is false; in fact I have explained precisely that this is what this formula means—that this is how one *does* say in this symbolic language that something that Prior says between t and t' is false. It also seems perfectly possible that I should enunciate this formula between t and t', and that I should do nothing else between t and t' that could possibly count as 'saying' anything. But we know by now what will happen if I do *that*; we know that whatever formula I enunciate during that period, I will not thereby say that something that I say is not the case, unless I also say something else during that period, which *ex hypothesi* I will not do.

This means that the very language in which these theorems are enunciated is one whose sentences cannot be used on some occasions to say the things which they can be used to say on other occasions. It is still not obvious, however, that this makes the language non-Tarskian; that is, it is not obvious that its metalanguage could not contain an expression 'true sentence' for which we would have, for every '$x$' which names a sentence of the language,

> $x$ is a true sentence if and only if $p$,

where '$p$' represents the translation of the sentence named by '$x$'. In particular, where '$N$' is the name of the sentence 'Something that Prior says between $t$ and $t'$ is not the case', there is nothing *obviously* wrong with anything that could be meant by

> $N$ is a true sentence if and only if something that Prior says between $t$ and $t'$ is not the case.

Note also that even if I use the sentence 'Something that Prior says between $t$ and $t'$ is not the case' to say, between $t$ and $t'$, that something that Prior says between $t$ and $t'$ is not the case, I'm not using this sentence of my language to talk about itself or about other sentences of my language; I'm using it to talk about what I say by it; so the hierarchy which Tarski demands is not broken down.

There is one line of inquiry, however, which I would like to mention, though not to pursue. I have been employing for some time a kind of informal metalogic in which I talk about using a sentence $S$ to say that $p$. Roughly, I think we use a sentence $S$ to say that $p$ if we use it with some degree of isolation, and the sentence means that $p$. The isolation has to be mentioned because we do not say that $p$ if we use a sentence that means that $p$, but use it as part of a longer sentence, e.g. we do not say that grass is pink by enunciating the sentence 'It is not the case that grass is pink' or 'If grass is pink I'll be jiggered'. At the same time, we can also get into trouble in some cases through *too much* isolation, as in the paradoxical cases we have been mulling over. Or perhaps in these cases the sentence doesn't *mean* what it ordinarily means. In any case this informal metalogic in which '$x$ means that $p$' is a fundamental form ought some time to be formalized. And we might be able, in such a metalogic, to define '$x$ is a true sentence' as '$x$ is a sentence, and for all $p$, if $x$ means that $p$, then $p$'. Whether truth thus defined would turn out to be Tarskian I don't know.

It is also worth seeing what would happen if we defied all the bans and made *this* metalanguage part of the language it is 'meta' to. At least some consequences of this are perfectly clear already. For '— means that —', like the Tarskian '— is a true sentence if and only if —', would be an expression of the sort that has figured largely in the preceding chapters, i.e. the sort that we have called 'a predicate at one end and a connective at the other', making a sentence from a name and a sentence. '*x* means that —' similarly resembles '*x* thinks that —', '*x* fears that —' and '*x* brings it about that —' in forming a sentence from a sentence; it will in fact be substitutable for 'δ' in all of the theorems set out symbolically in the last chapter. In particular we have, for any *x* whatever, such theorems as the following:

(1) If *x* means that something that *x* means is false, then something that *x* means *is* false.

(2) If *x* means that something that *x* means is false, then something that *x* means is true.

(3) If *x* means that something that *x* means is false, there are at least two distinct things that *x* means.

(4) If *x* means nothing except that something that *x* means is false, then it doesn't even mean that.

Note that the variable '*x*' here stands for an individual name— not for a 'name' of a *kind* of object, e.g. of a particular form of inscription, but for the name of an individual object, e.g. a particular inscription. Now it would generally be held that in a well-organized language each correctly formed sentence would have precisely one meaning; or even if different inscriptions or utterances of 'the same sentence' (i.e. in Peirce's language, the same sentence *type*) might have slightly different meanings (e.g. 'He's not here' said in different places about different people), still at least a particular single inscription or utterance ought to have precisely one meaning. Either, therefore, we must admit that our language is *not* as well organized as this; or we must deduce from (3) and (4) that *nothing* can mean that something that it means is false, i.e. that for no *x* can *x* mean that something that *x* means is false, or in other words, whatever inscribed sentence *x* might be, *x* does not mean that something that *x* means is false.

Suppose, however, that we arbitrarily assign the proper name 'Baf' to a certain series of black marks on white paper, namely the series of marks which constitute the last six words in the second sentence in this paragraph. Baf does not mean that something that Baf means is false. But if those last six words, i.e. the inscription Baf, do not mean (in the language we are now using —this is understood whenever we use the word 'mean' in the present discussion) that something that Baf means is false, they do not mean anything. But in any well-organized language, if a sub-sentence of a complex sentence has no meaning, neither has the sentence as a whole. From this it would follow that the second sentence in this paragraph, which appears to mean that Baf does not mean that something that Baf means is false, itself has no meaning.

In any case we gain nothing by following up this line, as one motive for looking into this is to see if we can construct a language in which a sentence-name $x$ *can* at least sometimes mean that $x$ is false; so it may be worth looking again at the alternative that we first put aside—that sentences of this language have more than one meaning at once. At any rate, writers like Buridan have explored this possibility, and have suggested, for instance, that whatever else a sentence $x$ may mean it always *also* means that it, $x$, is true. We could then say that if $x$ means that $x$ is false, it will have two contradictory meanings—that it is false and that it is true—and will be simply and non-paradoxically false. But we have to be careful here. We can't, for example, distinguish in such a case between the *principal* meaning of $x$ and its other meaning or meanings; for then we could use '$x$ principally means that' for the '$\delta$' of our theorems, and prove such things as that $x$ cannot principally mean that something that $x$ principally means is false unless it principally means something else as well, and then we're back where we started. So on the whole the prospects of a language containing its own semantics still don't look too bright.

My theorems *certainly* hold for Tarskian languages. Let $d = $ '$S$ is a sentence which is Tarskian-true if and only if . . .'. And this Tarski not only admits but insists on. My theorem will be in his metalanguage.

*If $S$ is a sentence [of $L$] which is T-true iff for some $p$, $S$ is a sentence [of $L$] which is T-true iff $p$, and it is not the case that $p$, then* *for some p, S is a sentence which is T-true iff p, and it is not the case that p.*

Or contrariwise:

If for no *p* is it true that (*S* is a sentence which is *T*-true iff *p*, and not *p*) then *S* is not a sentence which is *T*-true iff for some *p* etc.

$CN\Sigma pKE(s\epsilon Tr)pNpNE(s\epsilon Tr)\Sigma pKE(s\epsilon Tr)pNp.$

And the italicized bits won't be sentences of *L* and won't be *T*-true or *T*-false.[1]

---

[1] [This paragraph, which appears to us to supply a fitting end to a chapter which is partly fragmentary in the MS., is supplied from a MS. note dated 21/4/65.]

# PART II

# WHAT WE THINK ABOUT

# 8

## INTENTIONAL ATTITUDES AND RELATIONS

1. *'Thinking of' as a genuine relation*. From objects of thought in the sense of 'what we think', we may now at last turn to objects of thought in the more natural sense of what we think *of* or *about*. The first thing to be said here is that, prima facie at least, we *are* now concerned with a 'relation' in the strict sense. There is no question here, at all events not immediately, of a function of which one argument is a name and the other a sentence. 'Richard is thinking of Joan' is a sentence constructed from two genuine names, 'Richard' and 'Joan', by means of the two-place predicate '— is thinking of —'; the sentence is about Richard, but it is also about Joan, since it tells us that she is being thought of by Richard.

It is true, of course, that thinking *that y ɸ's* is one way of thinking of or about *y*, e.g. thinking that Joan is beautiful is one way of thinking about Joan. But this connection between the topics of thinking *of* and thinking *that* is a straightforward one, with plenty of parallel cases in the general logic of two-place predicates. It has already been pointed out that although, in 'Grass is green and the sky is blue', the conjunction 'and' is not a two-place predicate, and does not express a relation, it is nevertheless a component of the two-place predicate '— is green and — is blue', which does express a relation of colour-contrast, and this relation *is* asserted by the given sentence to hold between grass and the sky. It has also been pointed out that although the rather curious link '— is green, and —' is not a two-place predicate, and does not express a relation, it forms part of the same two-place predicate '— is green, and — is blue', expressing a relation of colour-contrast. The same may be said of other functors, such as '— thinks that —', of which one argument is a name and the other a sentence. These too may be part of genuine two-place predicates expressing relations between the objects denoted by two names. For example, '—believes that — is a Communist' is a two-place predicate expressing a relation that might hold between, say, Paul Jones and Elmer Gantry, i.e. the relation of 'attributing Communism to'. This point was, indeed, already made, in a preliminary way, in Chapter 2.

All the same, there are strong reasons for *not* regarding 'X is thinking of Y' as expressing a relation between X and Y.[1]


'Thinking about Peter is a *relation* between the thinker and Peter.' Let's go along with this for a bit, and make some contrasts. Does thinking about nobody express a relation between the thinker and nobody? Yes, if 'nobody' is understood in the same way in both occurrences, i.e. if 'thinking about nobody' means 'not thinking about anybody', and 'expressing a relation between the thinker and nobody' means 'not expressing a relation between the thinker and anybody'. And thus understood, of course, this *isn't* a case of the same thing as thinking about Peter, but rather a case of the opposite.

What about 'thinking about somebody'? It depends. The only *normal* way of using 'I am thinking about somebody' is to mean 'There is somebody that I am thinking about', i.e. 'For some *x*, I am thinking about *x*'—Peter, for instance. But it *might* be said, a little perversely, that I am 'thinking about somebody' if I am thinking that there's somebody in the next room, i.e. *not* thinking *of* somebody that *he* is in the next room, but just thinking *that there's somebody there*—that it's not empty of people. In this case I'm thinking about the room, but not thinking about the somebody that's there—maybe there *isn't* anybody there (I can still think there is, and be wrong). 'For some *x*, I think that $\phi x$' says that for some *x*, there is this relation between me and *x*; but 'I think that (for some *x*, $\phi x$)' doesn't say that there's any relation between me and anyone at all. If there *is* somebody in the room then there is *a* relation between me and him, viz. he is the one whose being in the room makes my thought true; but my thinking that there's somebody there isn't *itself* a relation between me and him, or between me and anybody. The relation that there is between me and him is one that is as it were outside my thought, like the relation between me and the word 'room' that I also have in these circumstances—if I think there is someone in the next room, then what I think is normally expressed in English by a sentence containing the word 'room', and *this* relation holds between me and that word. But my *thinking that etc.* isn't *itself* this relation (or any relation) to the word 'room'; maybe I am French, and think in French, but I still think something that is normally expressed in English by a sentence containing the word 'room'.—And of course if there *is* somebody in the next room then he stands to me in the relation of being in the next room to me; but my thinking that there is somebody etc. isn't this relation either (obviously).

If, then, I'm thinking there's somebody in the next room, I'm not thinking *about* the person who is there, if there is one; and still more obviously (though not more truly) I'm not thinking about the person who is there if there isn't one. In fact, in either case, I'm not thinking about anyone. Thought doesn't *have* to have an object, in the sense of 'that which is thought about', though it does have to have an object (or rather a pseudo-object!) in the sense of 'that which is thought' (cf. p. 3). Not all thinking is thinking-about.—But is *any*?

Suppose, still, that I think there is somebody in the next room, but don't know who this is, or even speculate about it; so that there is still no one of whom I think that *he* is in the next room. But suppose I go on to think that *the person in the next room* is making a dickens of a row, that he (*he*) ought to be spoken to about it, that he is a teddy-boy, etc. Am I not *now* 'thinking about the person in the next room'? and so is there not *now* an *x* such that I am thinking about *x*? (viz.: the person in the next room).—But what if there's no person there (but just a tape-recorder, or a machine, or nothing at all, but just a noise in my ears)?

Again, suppose I think there's somebody who stole my pencil —I don't know who, I don't speculate about it; there's no one of whom I think that *he* stole my pencil. But I go on to think that he's now in the next room. Is there not *now* somebody of whom I think that *he* is in the next room—an *x* such that I think that *x* is in the next room? (viz.: the person who stole my pencil).— But what if nobody stole my pencil (I just lost it)?

But if we answer 'no' to these questions, is there *ever* an *x* such that I think that $\phi x$?—is there *ever* anything that I think about? —does my thinking that $\phi x$ *ever* constitute a relation between me and some *x*? If *these* aren't cases of thinking about something, thinking *of* some *x* that $\phi x$, what *are* cases of this?

What's wrong with them? 'I am to the left of *x*'→'*x* is to the right of me'. But 'I think that the person who stole my pencil is in the next room'+→'The person who stole my pencil is thought by me to be in the next room'. For the first doesn't entail that someone stole my pencil, while the second does. But does 'I think that Peter is in the next room'→'Peter is thought by me to be in the next room'? Couldn't the first, but not the second, be true if Peter is someone in whose existence I have been persuaded to believe, but who in fact *doesn't* exist?

There are these possibilities:

(1) If anything, say *x*, actually exists (but not otherwise) I can think things *of x*.

(2) If anything, say *x*, is infallibly known by me to exist (but not otherwise) I can think things *of x*.

(3) If anything, say *x*, is believed by me to exist (but not otherwise) I can think things of *x*.

(4) I can think things *of* anything whatsoever.

Roughly, to anticipate, 'think of' is ambiguous; in one sense of it (2) is true, and in another, (4).

If (1) is true, I may think that I am thinking something of *x*, but in fact not be thinking something of *x*, because there is no *x*, and this entails that to think that I am thinking something of *x* is *not*, itself, *ipso facto* thinking something of *x* (viz. that I am thinking something of *x*).—Or does it? It might be said that I can only be *really* thinking that I am thinking something of *x*, just as I can only be *really* thinking something of *x*, if *x* exists. But by similar reasoning, one would be precluded from saying 'P thinks that he thinks that he is thinking something of *x*, but he can't really think that he is thinking something of *x*, because *x* doesn't exist'; for if *x* doesn't exist, I can't, either, think that I think that I am thinking something of *x*. So we can't be deluded about this (or our error can't be stated!—'whereof we cannot speak' etc.), and this would slide into (2).

But *dozens* of people would say that there's nothing *wrong* with denying that to think that one is thinking something of $x$ is itself thinking something of $x$. What *is* wrong with it? Well, write '$y$ is thinking something of $x$' as $\Sigma\phi Ty\phi x$, 'For some $\phi$, $y$ thinks that $\phi x$'. And we have

1. $CTy\phi x\Sigma\phi Ty\phi x$.
2. $CTy\Sigma\phi Ty\phi x\Sigma\phi Ty\phi x$
   $(= 1.\phi'/\Sigma\phi Ty\phi')$.

We can't get out of this except by fiendish restrictions on substitution for '$\phi$'.

If (3) is true, I can really think that $\phi x$, because I believe that $x$ exists, and yet Percy can't think that I think that $\phi x$, because he *doesn't* believe that $x$ exists. Only someone who shares a man's existential beliefs can think what that man's other thoughts are. Suppose we try to get round this thus: 'I know that Joe believes that there is a unique present King of France, and that Joe believes that *he* is bald.' How does this expand? 'I know that Joe believes that for some $x$, $x$ is the unique present King of France, and I know that Joe believes that $x$ is bald.' How am I using this last '$x$'? Not as a name—I can't. As a description? If so, what I here claim to 'know' *isn't* the thing that Joe *really* believes, for what Joe believes isn't just that *something* uniquely answers to a certain description and is bald—he believes *of* something that *it* is bald (*ex hypothesi*). If my '$x$' is a variable, it's a dangling one, for it's outside the scope of the 'for some $x$' in the earlier clause. It's nothing at all.

Isn't (2) open to a similar objection? Similar, yes; but not the same, and not as bad. If Joe infallibly knows that $x$ exists, he can believe *of* $x$ that $\phi x$, while *I* (if I don't share this knowledge) cannot believe *of* $x$ even that Joe believes *of* $x$ that $\phi x$. Still, I *can* believe that there is *an* $x$ such that Joe believes *of* $x$ that $\phi x$. And if I *don't* believe this (not only don't know it), then I can't believe that Joe *really* believes *of* any $x$ that $\phi x$. I may be wrong about this; but I can know exactly wherein my mistake consists, if I am mistaken.

Only (4) puts everyone on a level; but perhaps only by making the level pretty low. It amounts to saying that in '$x$ believes of $y$ that $\phi y$', this is *never* a genuine relation between $x$ and $y$, but *always* part of a story of the form

'$x$ believes that for some $y$, . . . and $\phi y$ . . .'.

And we may combine this with (1), the sense of 'believes of' for which (1) holds, call it 'BELIEVES OF', being defined in terms of the other as follows:

$x$ BELIEVES OF $z$ that $\phi z$
$= x$ believes that for some $y$, $\psi y$ . . . and $\phi y$ . . .;
and in fact $\psi z$ . . . and $\phi z$ . . .[1]

which does express a genuine relation between $x$ and $z$. And '$x$ BELIEVES OF $z$ that $\phi z$' entails '$x$ BELIEVES OF $z$ that $x$ BELIEVES of $z$ that $\phi z$' if '$x$ believes that $p$' entails '$x$ believes that $x$ believes that $p$'.

2. *Reid on the possible unreality and generality of objects of thought.* There is a point of view according to which the sort of problems I have been considering arise simply from trying to force attitude-statements into a mould which they will not fit; if we would only take them as they come, it is suggested, and detail their characteristics as they actually present themselves to us, we would get into much less trouble. The classic statement of this point of view is that in Thomas Reid's *Essays on the Intellectual Powers of Man*, which I shall compare with one or two more recent versions.

In Essay II, 'Of the powers we have by means of our external senses', Reid has a chapter (Ch. 11) on 'Bishop Berkeley's sentiments of the nature of ideas', at the end of which he says:

In perception, in remembrance, and in conception, or imagination, I distinguish three things—the mind that operates, the operation of the mind, and the object of that operation. That the object perceived is one thing, and the perception of that object another, I am as certain as I can be of anything. The same may be said of conception, of remembrance, of love and hate, of desire and aversion. In all these, the act of the mind about the object is one thing, the object is another thing. There must be an object, real or imaginary, distinct from the operation of the mind about it.

This is one of Reid's 'master-theses'; we shall find him returning to it again and again. He uses it at this point merely to distinguish perception, etc. from sensation—things, I suppose, like feeling itchy—which he says involves nothing but the affected mind and the sensation affecting it. We might be tempted to say that for Reid sensation is a *quality* of the mind, while perception,

---

[1] [The MS reads thus, but 'and $\phi z$' is surely an oversight.]

memory, and conception are *relations* to something else, but we would do well to resist this temptation—in Reid's successors, at all events, it is just this sort of categorization which we are warned to avoid. And already in Reid, it seems to be blocked by what I would call his second 'master-thesis'. This is hinted at in the 'real or imaginary' in the last sentence of the above quotation; it begins to emerge more explicitly in his treatment of memory. He repeats that 'memory must have an object', for 'every man who remembers must remember something, and that which he remembers is called the object of his remembrance'. 'Every man can distinguish the thing remembered from the remembrance of it.' So far, 'memory agrees with perception'. But 'the object of memory, or thing remembered, must be something that is past'. 'What now is, cannot be an object of memory.' And with 'conception', he has a still more emphatic point to make:

That which essentially distinguishes it from every other power of the mind . . . is, that it is not employed solely about things which have existence. I can conceive a winged horse or centaur, as easily and distinctly as I can conceive a man whom I have seen . . .

The powers of sensation, of perception, of memory and of consciousness [i.e. introspection] are all employed solely about objects that do exist, or have existed. But conception is often employed about objects that neither do, nor did, nor will exist. This is the very nature of this faculty, that its object, though distinctly conceived, may have no existence.

So far from seeing any conflict between his two 'master-theses', Reid uses the first to support the second, or at least to clear away a possible source of objections to it. It is precisely because 'we must distinguish between that act, or operation of the mind, which we call conceiving an object, and the object which we conceive', that we can say without contradiction that although the former must exist, the latter need not.

Reid also says that the object of conception may be *general* or *universal* in a sense in which no existing object, and in particular no *act* of conception, can be so.

Suppose I conceive a triangle—that is, a plane figure terminated by three right lines. He that understands this definition directly, has a distinct conception of a triangle. But a triangle is not an individual; it is a species. The act of my understanding in conceiving is an individual act, and has a real existence; but the thing conceived is general, and cannot exist without other attributes, which are not included in the definition.

Every triangle that really exists must have a certain length of sides and measure of angles; it must have place and time. But the definition of a triangle includes neither existence nor any of these attributes; and therefore they are not included in the conception of a triangle, which cannot be accurate if it comprehend more than the definition.

This is not perhaps very happily put. The sentence 'A triangle is not an individual; it is a species' grates particularly on the modern ear, and would send some people rushing for quotation-marks. But it is certainly not obvious that Reid is talking about the phrase 'a triangle' here; he is, rather, caught up in a similar tangle to that which set Frege saying 'The concept *horse* is not a concept, it is an object'—except that it set Reid saying the opposite unsatisfactory thing; what he says is more like 'A horse (or a triangle) is not an object, it is a concept.' Reid's successors (and Frege's) have found better ways of making the same point; but we shall return to this.

3. *Reid and others against 'Ideas'*. Returning to his main point, the possible non-existence of what we conceive, Reid apologizes for 'insisting upon a point so very evident as that men may barely conceive things that never existed', but explains that he has to do so because of a prevalent 'prejudice' among philosophers 'that in all the operations of the understanding, there must be an object of thought, which really exists while we think of it'. This prejudice has led philosophers to postulate two objects of thought where 'the vulgar' can only find one. 'The philosopher says, Though there may be a remote object which does not exist, there must be an immediate object which really exists; for that which is not, cannot be an object of thought.' Philosophers have been thus 'led to think that, in every act of memory and of conception, . . . there are two objects—the one, the immediate object, the idea, . . .; the other, the mediate or external object.' Besides making a distinction where there is none, Reid says, this theory prevents us from making distinctions which we can all see to be genuine.

The philosopher says, I cannot conceive a centaur without having an idea of it in my mind. . . . He surely does not mean that I cannot conceive it without conceiving it. That would make me no wiser. What then is this idea? Is it an animal, half horse and half man? No. Then I am certain it is not the thing I conceive . . .

This one object which I conceive is not the image of an animal—it is an animal. I know what it is to conceive an image of an animal, and what it is to conceive an animal; and I can distinguish the one of these from the other without any danger of mistake.

The theory that Reid is attacking here is now a dead one, and it has been killed precisely by this argument, either in Reid's hands or in those of others. Reid's argument is echoed, for instance, in Russell's remark:

> To say that unicorns have an existence in heraldry, or in literature, or in imagination, is a most pitiful and paltry evasion. What exists in heraldry is not an animal, made of flesh and blood, moving and breathing of its own initiative. What exists is a picture, or a description in words.[1]

—and that isn't what a unicorn is.

J. S. Mill also comes very close to making Reid's point when he attacks Hobbes's theory that names are names of our ideas or conceptions rather than of the things conceived. Mill argues thus:

> Names are not intended only to make the hearer conceive what we conceive, but also to inform him what we believe. Now, when I use a name for the purpose of expressing a belief, it is a belief concerning the thing itself, not concerning my idea of it.[2]

And he repeats this point when he comes to consider 'the import of propositions':

> Propositions (except sometimes when the mind itself is the subject treated of) are not assertions respecting our ideas of things, but respecting the things themselves. In order to believe that gold is yellow, I must, indeed, have the idea of gold, and the idea of yellow . . .; but my belief has not reference to the ideas, it has reference to the things. . . . I cannot dig the ground unless I have the idea of the ground, and of a spade, and of all the other things I am operating upon. . . . But it would be a very ridiculous description of digging the ground to say that it is putting one idea into another. Digging is an operation which is performed upon the things themselves, though it

---

[1] B. A. W. Russell, *Introduction to Mathematical Philosophy*, p. 169.
[2] *System of Logic*, i. ii. 1.

cannot be performed unless I have in my mind the ideas of them. And in like manner, believing is an act which has for its subject the facts themselves, though a previous mental conception of the facts is an indispensable condition. When I say that fire causes heat, do I mean that my idea of fire causes my idea of heat? No: I mean that the natural phenomenon, fire, causes the natural phenomenon, heat. When I mean to assert anything respecting the ideas, I give them their proper name; I call them **ideas**; as when I say that a child's idea of a battle is unlike the reality . . .[1]

The comparison with digging puts as sharply as it could possibly be put the view that in believing something about an object we thereby put ourselves into as real a relation with that object as when we relate ourselves to it, or are related to it, physically. And his final point is exactly Reid's; I mean the point that we *are* in exceptional cases related to 'ideas' in the way in which we are normally related to other objects, and the very subsumption of this case under the general one, the contrasts with the other cases subsumable under it, makes it quite clear the 'relation to ideas' will not do as a description of the general case. Mill's point is nicely summed up by Johnson:

His dictum is that propositions are not about ideas, but about things: and by this he intended to assert that a proposition is concerned with the things it expressly talks of, and not with any mental process that may be involved in the assent to or understanding of the proposition. . . . This, of course, holds, whether the matter of the proposition is physical reality or mental reality: we must understand what is meant by the association of ideas or by an emotion of danger in a psychological proposition, just as we must understand what is meant by dragons or horses in propositions describing such creatures; while, on the other hand, the propositions in neither case are concerned with those processes of understanding.[2]

Johnson also makes the further point that one might well have expected Mill to make, namely that even the 'ideas' which Mill admits to be presupposed in believing (and for that matter in digging) are conceivings *of* real objects. Johnson says, almost epigrammatically: 'I agree that judgment relates the object of one thought to the object of another; but I deny that judgment relates the thought of one object to the thought of another.'[3]

[1] *System of Logic*, I. v. I.        [2] *Logic*, I. x. 3.        [3] Ibid. I. xiii. 8.

But while Johnson, in developing Mill's point, expressly mentions dragons, and Reid in anticipating it mentions centaurs, it is noteworthy that Mill himself keeps to safer ground, and when he does come to discuss dragons he seems to forget everything that he says in the passages just cited. Mill was worried by the syllogism:

A dragon is a thing which breathes flame;
A dragon is a serpent;
Therefore some serpent or serpents breathe flame

which on Aristotelian principles is valid. But instead of questioning the Aristotelian principles, he indulges in what Russell would no doubt describe as the 'pitiful and paltry evasion' of saying that if the syllogism is about real dragons, i.e. if its premisses mean

A dragon is a *really existing* thing which breathes flame, etc.,

then these premisses are false, and that the premisses which the propounders of the syllogism really intend are either

Dragon is a *word meaning* a thing which breathes flame, etc.

or

The *idea of* a dragon is *an idea of* a thing which breathes flame, etc.[1]

But if a dragon is not, really, a thing which breathes flame, would not an idea of one *as* a thing which breathes flame be a false and inaccurate one? What would he say about 'I would be frightened if a dragon came into this room'? Would he say that this was about a word or an idea (which would not frighten any normal person in the least)? His own principles should have taught him better than this.

4. *Brentano, Meinong, and Findlay on objects of thought.* Modern writers who echo Reid's first 'master-thesis' have generally caught it not from him but from Brentano. Looking for the distinguishing character of 'psychical phenomena', Brentano found it in what 'the Schoolmen of the Middle Ages called the intentional inexistence of an object', that is, 'direction to an

[1] *System of Logic*, I. viii. 5.

object (by which we need not understand a reality)', or 'an immanent objectivity'. He goes on, in this often-cited passage:

> Every mental state possesses in itself something which serves as an object, although not all possess their objects in the same way. In a presentation something is presented, in a judgment something is acknowledged or rejected, in love something is loved, in hate hated, in desire desired, etc.[1]

Brentano's most recent and perhaps most sympathetic expositor is J. N. Findlay, in his *Values and Intentions*. But before turning to this book, it is worth consulting his earlier book on Brentano's disciple Meinong.[2] Meinong maintained the 'paradoxical thesis' that 'the realm of objects is far wider than the realm of existents', and deplored the 'prejudice in favour of the actual' that led us to 'ignore the unreal and treat it as a mere nothing'. 'It is clear', Findlay says (expounding Meinong, and I think at this point agreeing with him), 'that we are able to think of objects that do not exist', and when we do so, 'the objects that are before us are undoubtedly something, they are distinct from the experiences by whose means they are given to us' (Reid's basic distinction again). Meinong's view is also that 'there are many true statements that we can make about' such objects; for example, 'though it is not a fact that the golden mountain . . . exists, he thinks that it is unquestionably a fact that the golden mountain is both golden and mountainous' (cf. Reid's insistence that the centaur he conceives 'is an animal'). Meinong is sometimes charged with crudely treating objects as 'beings' in a wide sense, and 'real' objects as a sub-species; but Findlay defends him against this, and says that his actual view was that 'the pure object stands beyond being and non-being', and 'whether an object is or not, makes no difference to *what* the object is'. Some objects of thought also stand beyond other dichotomies; these are the 'incomplete' objects which 'lie before us whenever we think, in a perfectly general way, of "something that is so-and-so"', and which 'do not possess any characteristics beyond those specified in their "so-and-so"' (cf. Reid on the conception of 'a triangle').[3]

---

[1] [*Psychologie vom empirischen Standpunkt*, II. i. 5.]
[2] [*Meinong's Theory of Objects and Values*, Oxford, 1963.]
[3] [Op. cit., pp. 43, 49, 156.]

Findlay in his own development of Brentano attaches particular importance to a passage in which Brentano holds 'the intentionality of mental states to be a case of a unique logical category: the category of a determination which is *relation-like* without being a proper case of a relation'. And it is Reid's second master-thesis that makes the main difference. Findlay suggests that 'intentionality . . . is a relational property which is one-sided, which does not involve the being of a corresponding relation or related term'. I am not sure how seriously he intends this description to be taken. Certainly 'thinking of T' is a 'property' of the thinker; and Findlay's comparison is with such properties as being taller than Y, which are formed by attaching a term to the relation of being taller than; only in 'thinking of Y' the property isn't *really* 'relational' at all, and it seems to be suggested that it is *not* analysable into a 'thinking of' part and a 'Y' part. In any case, it is

an incontestable fact that in describing a state of mind as being *of* this or *of* that, we must not be taken to imply that there *is* anything having the character attributed to [the] object. . . . From the fact that X is striking an F one can infer that something is an F, but from the fact that X is thinking of an F one cannot infer that there is some F of which X is thinking.[1]

There are other fallacious inferences, too, which would be justified if intentionality were a relation properly so called.

Because a term occupying the *object* position in an ordinary relational statement can . . . be shifted into a corresponding *subject* position—'Brutus killed a bald man' being transformed into 'A bald man was killed by Brutus'—it is thought that a similar transformation should be possible in the case of a statement involving mental reference—e.g. 'Brutus dreamt of a bald man' should yield 'Some bald man was dreamt of by Brutus'. . . . Because a term occupying an object position in an ordinary relational statement can be replaced by another term having an identical reference—'Brutus killed the author of *De Bello Gallico*' being replaceable by 'Brutus killed the husband of Calpurnia'—it is thought that the same should be possible in a statement concerning mental reference—e.g. 'Brutus thought of the author of the *De Bello Gallico*' and 'Brutus thought of the husband of Calpurnia'.[2]

[1] [*Values and Intentions*, p. 35.]    [2] [Ibid., p. 36.]

Because these transformations are clearly unwarranted (the last perhaps not so clearly, but it would be easy enough to make it so), 'it is thought that the whole statement requires reformulation, or an analysis into terms that will not yield these objectionable inferences'. But this enterprise, Findlay suggests, is misguided. Just as we have now learnt to live with genuine relations, and not attempt to reduce them to qualities, so we should learn to live with this other category, with its own 'unique but not puzzling' peculiarities.

The 'touchstone of the mental', Findlay says again, is its 'built-in reference to what is not part of it and to what need not exist anywhere at all', and he deplores

the notion that there is something intrinsically different between thinking and talking of what does, and of what does not exist, that thought or talk about what does not exist, should be said to be *about* something, or to refer to something, only in some derived, secondary or 'Pickwickian' fashion. . . . Whereas there is absolutely no *intrinsic* difference between thinking and talking about what does, and what does not really exist.[1]

This last is directed against Russell's 'theory of descriptions'; not entirely fairly, since (as we shall see later) one of the motivations of that theory was precisely to give an account of 'The so-and-so $\phi$'s', 'X thinks that the so-and-so $\phi$'s', etc. which gives them the same meaning—and in the second case the same truth-value—whether there is any such object as the so-and-so or not.

5. *Miss Anscombe on intentional objects.* Before making a serious critical examination of Findlay's position, or of Reid's, I want to mention one other writer who I think is also appealing to us to treat 'intentionality' as 'what it is, and not another thing'— Miss Anscombe, in her paper on 'The Intentionality of Sensation'.[2] Miss Anscombe seems to differ fairly sharply from Reid on the subject of sensation and perception, and to assimilate them more closely to what he calls 'conception' than he would allow; but I do not want to concentrate on this part of her paper so much as on her preliminary account of intentionality as such.

---

[1] [*Values and Intentions*, p. 42.]
[2] [In *Analytical Philosophy* (ed. R. J. Butler), 2nd series, pp. 158–80.]

She makes some useful remarks, to begin with, of an etymological character, and points out a curious reversal which has befallen the meanings of the words 'subject' and 'object':

> The subject used to be what the proposition, say, is about, the thing itself as it is in reality . . . ; objects on the other hand were formerly always objects *of* —. Objects of desire, objects of thought, are not objects in one common modern sense, not individual things, such as *the objects found in the accused man's pockets.*

She introduces the phrase 'intentional objects' for 'objects' in the old sense, which need not be 'objects' in the new sense at all. This obviously needs to be remembered if we are trying to make sense of Reid and Brentano, and perhaps even of Meinong (though here I am not sure).

'Intentional objects', then, may or may not be real. 'If I am thinking of Winston Churchill then he is the object of my thought. And I may worship the moon.'

> But now suppose the object of my thought is Mr. Pickwick . . . ; and the object of my worship is Zeus. . . . With the proper names I named no man and no god, since they name a fictitious man and a false god. Moreover, Mr. Pickwick and Zeus are nothing but a fictitious man and a false god (contrast the moon, which though a false god, is a perfectly good heavenly body). All the same it is clear that 'The Greeks worshipped Zeus' is true. Thus 'X worshipped —' and 'X thought of —' are not to be assimilated to 'X bit —'. For . . . the name of something real has to be put in the blank space in 'X bit —' if the completed sentence is to have so much as a chance of being true. Whereas in 'X worshipped —' and 'X thought of —' that is not so.

Miss Anscombe, like Reid, considers the 'not very happy move' of introducing 'ideas' as the real objects (in the modern sense) which fill in the blanks after 'intentional verbs'; and like Reid, objects to the suggestion that 'the *idea* is what X was worshipping or thinking of'. She also objects (like Findlay) that

> the mere fact of real existence . . . can't make so much difference to the analysis of a sentence like 'X thought of —'. So if the idea is to be brought in when the object doesn't exist, then equally it should be brought in when the object does exist. Yet one is thinking, surely, of Winston Churchill, not of the idea of him.

But this is not the only peculiarity of 'intentional objects'; another is what Miss Anscombe calls their 'indeterminacy':

> I can think of a man without thinking of a man of any particular height; I cannot hit a man without hitting a man of a particular height, because there is no such thing as a man of no particular height.

(Compare Reid on considering a triangle, and Meinong's 'incomplete' objects.) Similarly, if we ask 'What does the sentence "John sent Mary a book" say John sent Mary?' the answer is 'A book', but there is no answer to the question 'Which book?'

There is a third peculiarity which Miss Anscombe stresses, as Findlay does also, but not Reid. It is 'possible that when I am thinking of a particular man, not every true description of him is one under which I am thinking of him'. She no doubt has in mind here the stock cases of what is sometimes called 'referential opacity', a topic which will be considered more fully in the next chapter. Tom may be thinking of Tully, i.e. of Cicero, and yet may not be thinking of him *as* Tully, but as Cicero (he may not know that Tully is Cicero). And at this point Miss Anscombe introduces a distinction which Reid quite signally failed to notice. She takes a case in which 'a man aims at a stag, but the thing that he took for a stag was his father'. There seems in such a case to be clearly a sense in which he aimed at his father, and a sense in which he did not. The 'intentional object' of his aiming, i.e. what he was trying or preparing to shoot, was a stag (he was trying or preparing to shoot a stag). But the object at which his gun was pointing was in fact his father; Miss Anscombe says that his father was the 'material object' of his aiming. Similarly a tribe may be 'worshipping a god', though what they are worshipping is in fact 'a mere hunk of wood'; the intentional object of their worship would then be a non-existent god, and its material object an existent piece of wood. Sometimes in such a situation one can find an intentional object which is also a material object, e.g. the man might aim, and intend to aim, at a 'dark patch against the foliage', which he took to be a stag but was in fact his father, but which in any case was really there. Sometimes this is not possible, as when a man is 'totally hallucinated' and shooting at 'something in his hallucinatory scene', or when 'there is no description, still giving the intentional object of worship, which describes any-thing actual', so that 'the worshippers, materially speaking, worship a nothing, something that does not exist'. Even in this last case, however, Miss Anscombe gives a caution:

> Not that it will then do to say 'They worship nothing', but only: 'What they worship is nothing'. For 'They worship nothing' would imply that no sentence 'They worship such-and-such' will be true; and in the case supposed some such sentence is true.

6. *Difficulties in these views.* One cannot help feeling—the feeling comes most acutely as one reads the last-quoted passage from Miss Anscombe—that all these writers are walking on a tight-rope; though Reid in particular contrives to suggest that it's quite a low and thick one, and that you don't have to be much of an acrobat to toddle along it quite easily. But it just *isn't* as easy as all that. For it just isn't easy to hold together the follow-ing two propositions:

(1) That when X thinks of Y, aims at Y, worships Y, etc., there is always a Y involved as well as an X.

(2) That in some cases, when X thinks of Y, etc., there is no Y there at all.

Or, at least, it isn't easy to hold them together and at the same time to reject all of the following moves which might make them consistent:

(a) That thinking of an unreal object is quite a different sort of activity from thinking of a real one.

(b) That in thinking of anything at all, we thereby put our-selves into a relation, not with *that thing,* but only with an 'idea' or what-have-you which in favourable cases may 'represent' a real thing but in unfavourable ones does not.

(c) That there are strong and weak kinds of reality or being, such that all objects of thought whatever possess at least the weak sort, while only a favoured sub-class possess the strong sort.

Certainly (1) and (2) are both plausible, and (a), (b), and (c) are not, but to say that we *must* hold firm to (1) and (2) and yet *must* avoid the evasions (a), (b), and (c), is in the end to state a problem rather than to solve it. Still, state it these writers did;

the problem is there, and we must see what further, if anything, can be done about it.[1]

In all of the three writers we have just discussed—most explicitly in Findlay, but also in the other two—there is the suggestion that there is nothing really puzzling or complicated about thinking of or about something, if only we will just take this for what it is and not try and make it out to be a special case of something else, and if only, in particular, we do not try to subsume it under the familiar logical heading of a 'relation'. When, however, we look more closely at the pure phenomenology of the matter as presented by these writers, it does, I am afraid, present puzzles and paradoxes which are not so easily swept aside.

In the first place, how seriously are we to take the united insistence of Reid, Findlay, and Miss Anscombe that 'thinking of' must always have an *object*? At the very least this would seem to mean that it is no mere linguistic accident that the form 'X is thinking of Y' has three distinct parts—three distinct dimensions of variation, or slots into which we can put alternative elements. In the first place, the thinker may not be X but some other; but at this point there are no obvious puzzles and we may in the meantime forget it. Then 'is thinking of' may be replaced, if not by any other relational expression, at least by any other 'intentional' verb, such as 'is talking about', or 'has hopes for', or 'intends to shoot'. And Y may be replaced by some other 'object'; moreover, this replacement makes a significant difference even if both objects are non-existent; it is one thing to be thinking of Mr. Pickwick, and quite another thing to be thinking of Mr. Churchill.

On the other hand, there is a suggestion in both modern writers, and possibly in Reid too, that the third element in this complex is somehow 'inseparable' from the second. In the case of Miss Anscombe, it sometimes seems as if she is merely making a point about the grammar of the word 'object', in its older sense—the point, precisely, that 'object' in this sense is a *relative* term; that a thing can no more be a mere object without being an object *of* something, than it can be merely shorter without

---

[1] [What follows, to the end of the chapter, is taken from an incomplete alternative draft of Chapter 9.]

being shorter *than* something. But I think there's more to it than this, even for Miss Anscombe, and there certainly is for Findlay. The suggestion is perhaps that 'thinking of Y' and 'thinking of Z' are simply different *ways* of thinking, different *modifications* of this activity, in a totally peculiar sense, not to be assimilated to the sense in which being Richard's father is one way of being a father and being John's father is another, but more like, say, the difference between thinking slowly and thinking fast.

Miss Anscombe, however, also insists—and one has the feeling that Reid, if not Findlay, would also insist—that if what one thinks of happens also to exist, as in the case of Mr. Churchill, then what one thinks of just *is* the very object that one might also, for instance, bite or shave. The name 'Winston Churchill', in other words, functions in exactly the same way as in 'X is thinking of Winston Churchill' as it does in 'X is biting Winston Churchill'; it serves to *refer* to an actual object, in the modern sense, which happens also to be an object (in the old sense) of thought. Winston Churchill doesn't have to be transformed into, or replaced by, something else (the 'idea' of him) in order to be thought of. But then, surely, 'X is thinking of Winston Churchill *is* of the same form as 'X is biting Mr. Churchill'—a couple of names linked by a two-place predicate.

But then Miss Anscombe says that 'the mere fact of real existence . . . can't make so much difference to the analysis of a sentence like "X thought of —"'; and Findlay is very strong on this too: 'There is absolutely no *intrinsic* difference between thinking and talking about what does and what does not really exist.' This surely means that the grammar of 'X thought of —' is exactly the same in the two cases, so that if we have a couple of referring expressions and a two-place predicate in the one case we have it in the other, and if not in the one, then not in the other. Miss Anscombe appeals to this principle in her argument against the 'idea' theory: if it's Mr. Churchill and not just an idea of him that we are thinking of, then it's Mr. Pickwick and not an idea of him that we are thinking of. Perhaps the principle that the two cases are alike doesn't *need* to be appealed to here; it is surely obvious in any case, as Reid saw, that to think of X is one thing and to think of an idea or image of X is another thing, and the difference is especially obvious when X itself doesn't exist but the idea or image does. But it would certainly be awkward to say that thinking of X *isn't* the same sort of thing when X exists and when it doesn't; for a man might well think of X, and know perfectly well what it is for him to be thinking of X, without knowing whether X exists or not; and a third party might think that Y is thinking of X, and know perfectly well what he is taking Y to be doing, without knowing whether X exists or not.

(*a*) X's thinking of Y constitutes a relation between X and Y when Y exists, but (*b*) not when Y doesn't; but (*c*) X's thinking of Y is the same sort of thing whether Y exists or not. Something plainly has to be given up here; what will it be?

# 9

## GENERAL AND INDIVIDUAL
## THOUGHTS

1. *The grammar of having in mind.* Let us go back to the beginning. We are considering what happens when the object of X's thought is Y, i.e. when X is thinking about Y. This is not wholly unconnected with our first sense of 'object of thought', i.e. the sense in which this phrase means *what we think* when we *think that* so-and-so. For if X thinks about Y, then either always or at least usually there must be *something that* X thinks about Y; let us confine ourselves to this case in the meantime, i.e. to the case in which 'X is thinking *something* about Y'. We also have the form 'X *thinks* something about Y', expressing a 'dispositional' rather than an 'occurrent' thinking. We will let our reflections cover this case also; the difference between dispositional and occurrent thinking is no doubt important, but I don't think it has any bearing on the set of problems with which we are now concerned.

'X thinks something about Y' appears to be an existential generalization of more specific statements of the form 'X thinks about Y that . . .'; or as we might more often say, 'X thinks *of* Y that . . .'. For example, 'Othello thinks of' (or 'about') 'Desdemona that she loves Cassio'. We are concerned here, in fact, with a three-argument function (or functional expression) in which two of the arguments are names and the third is something like a sentence. In fact it is not quite that, in any but the most crassly grammatical sense of 'sentence'. For only looking at the rest of the larger sentence will tell us who the 'she' is in 'she loves Cassio'; this sub-sentence has, as Keynes used to say,[1] 'no independent import'. The functional expression with which we have to deal here is in fact '— thinks of — that she —'; at least, this is what we have to do with apart from the logically irrelevant indication of sex in 'she'. The expression constructs

[1] J. M. Keynes, *Formal Logic*, 4th ed., p. 251.

a sentence from a name, another name, and a verb, and is equivalent to '— thinks that — —'; for example, 'Othello thinks of Desdemona that she loves Cassio' just boils down to 'Othello thinks that Desdemona loves Cassio'.

But if *this* is how this expression constructs a sentence from a name, another name, and a verb, I mean if the second name and the verb hitch into their places in *this* way, what is the difference between this and constructing a sentence from a name and a sentence, or between this '— thinks that — —' and our original '— thinks that —'? None at all, I would suggest; '$x$ thinks that $y$ $\phi$'s' *is* just the special case of '$x$ thinks that $p$' in which '$p$' is '$y$ $\phi$'s', and the 'thinks that' is the same in both. We get something really new only when the verb-gap is filled in and the name-gap isn't. We then get a two-place predicate, such as '— thinks of — that she loves Cassio', or the equivalent '— thinks that — loves Cassio' (or '— ascribes loving Cassio to —').

This apparently pointless separation of a verb from its subject, and subsequent supplying of a quasi-subject to expand the verb into something like a sentence, may be encountered in other contexts too. In particular, the simple '$x$ $\phi$'s', e.g. 'Desdemona is faithful', may be expanded to 'It is true of $x$ that it $\phi$'s', e.g. 'It is true of Desdemona that she is faithful'. What is going on here is partly the old game of 'nominalizing'; a 'that' is introduced in a position where it is tempting to see it as forming the name of an abstract object. '*What* does Othello think of Desdemona? That she is unfaithful.' '*What* is true of Desdemona? That she is faithful.' Often, indeed, these 'that' clauses with pronouns are interchangeable, or almost interchangeable, with more familiar quasi-names of *abstracta*. This comes out very sharply if we re-examine Cook Wilson's classic chapter on 'Subject and Predicate'.[1]

Cook Wilson observes that although it is traditionally said that the predicate is what we say of the subject, in the sentence 'Jones is musical' we would in practice say that the predicate is 'is musical', but not that what is said of Jones is 'is musical'; what is said to be said of Jones would be rather 'that he is musical'. On the other hand, Cook Wilson goes on, what is said to be 'predicated' of Jones would be neither 'is musical' nor 'that he is musical', but 'musicalness'. But the difference

---

[1] [*Statement and Inference*, Part II, Ch. IV, 55, pp. 114–17.]

between 'musicalness' and 'that he is musical' is not very great, and there are certainly contexts in which they may be used indifferently, e.g. 'Musicalness is a characteristic of Jones', 'That he is musical is a characteristic of Jones'. The two forms are related very much as 'The conquest of Gaul by Caesar' and 'That Caesar conquered Gaul'; 'was denied by X' could follow either of these. Cook Wilson identifies what is said to be said of Jones, 'that he is musical', with 'that Jones is musical'; but this is inaccurate. The true relation between the two is that to say *of* Jones that *he* is musical is to say (*tout court*) that *Jones* is musical; or to use the other forms: to *ascribe* musicalness to Jones is to *assert* Jones's musicalness.

The suggestion of an abstract *designatum* is here, as always, a trick, whether it be done by '-ness' suffixes or 'that' prefixes. But the expansion of the simple verb to a quasi-sentence need not be misleading, and I'm not sure that it is always even dispensable. A verb *is* like a sentence; its job is to make sentences from names, and it is rather like a sentence with gaps in it; and above all, verbs may be compounded in exactly the same way as sentences may; or better, every compounding of sentences is *ipso facto* a compounding of such verbs as they contain. '— is green and — is blue' is as good a verb, or anyway as good a 'two-place predicate', as '— shaves —'. In these complex cases, to isolate the predicate without using blanks, we do need variables or pronouns or expressions like 'the former' and 'the latter' ('Grass and the sky', we might say, 'are such that the former is green and the latter is blue').

These are everyday-speech devices that are rather like the symbolic 'abstracts' discussed in Chapter 3; we cannot do without them but their use need not involve us, any more than the use of 'abstracts' need involve us, in any 'Platonizing', i.e. seriously intended nominalizing of verbs and similar forms. And the collapsing of the form 'It is true of $x$ that it $\phi$'s' into the plain '$x$ $\phi$'s' is the everyday-speech counterpart of the collapsing of $(\lambda y \phi y)x$ into $\phi x$, while that of 'X believes of Y that she is unfaithful' into 'X believes that Y is unfaithful' is a similar collapsing of something that we might write as $B(x, y, \lambda z \phi z)$ into $Bx\phi y$. But I do not wish to carry this parallel with abstraction-operators too far. The cases discussed in Chapter 3 for which 'abstracts' seemed indispensable were rather recondite ones;

but the cases in which we seem unable to do without the corresponding ordinary-speech devices are not at all recondite, and it is not evident that their symbolic representation requires the device of abstraction; what it does require is the careful use of quantifiers.

2. *Quantification inside and outside belief-contexts*. The expanded locutions we have been considering are scarcely dispensable once quantifications are introduced. 'Othello thinks of *someone* that she is unfaithful' does *not* mean the same as 'Othello thinks *that someone is unfaithful*'. He could think the latter thought without particularizing—he could just believe that there *are* instances of infidelity without even mentally accusing anyone in particular of it—but to say that he thinks of someone that *she* is unfaithful is to say that he *does* think this of someone in particular.

This is simply an extension to belief-functions and the like of a distinction with which ordinary logic is perfectly familiar in the case of negation. Ordinary speech, indeed, rather slides about here when the word 'someone' is used. 'It is not the case that someone is unfaithful' is unclear in ordinary speech; it *ought* to mean that the proposition that someone is unfaithful is false, i.e. that no one is unfaithful, but I'm not sure that that is how it would be ordinarily understood—it might well be understood as a mere turning-around of the other thing, i.e. 'There is someone of whom it is not the case that she is unfaithful', i.e. not 'No one is unfaithful' but 'Someone is not'. (Even 'Othello thinks that someone is unfaithful' has a similar unclarity.) In ordinary speech we tend to change a 'someone' which does not govern but is governed by a 'not' into 'anyone'—to make 'It is not the case that (someone is unfaithful)' unambiguous. We say 'It is not the case that *anyone* is unfaithful', or just '*Not anyone* is unfaithful'; 'Not (someone is unfaithful)' we don't use. However, the distinction that needs to be made is clear enough, and logicians do it by writing 'It is not the case that (for some $x$ ($x$ is unfaithful))' in the one case and 'For some $x$ (it is not the case that ($x$ is unfaithful))' in the other. Similarly 'Othello believes that (for some $x$ ($x$ is unfaithful))' is to be distinguished from 'For some $x$ (Othello believes that ($x$ is unfaithful))'.

It was said earlier that Othello's ascription of infidelity to some particular person, say Desdemona, i.e. his believing (or saying) that that person is unfaithful, constitutes a *relation* between Othello and that person, although 'believing that' on its own does not express a relation (it is not a two-place predicate, but a 'predicate at one end and connective at the other'). It was also noted that there are cases where 'believing that' does not even enter into the composition of a relation; namely where what is believed is not *about* anything, and its verbal expression does not contain a *name* of anything. These are precisely the cases that we are beginning to consider now, and compare more closely with the others. It is obvious that if Othello believes that *no one* is unfaithful, this does not constitute a relation between Othello and anyone at all. This is equally the case, though not perhaps so obviously so, if Othello simply believes *that someone is unfaithful*, i.e. that someone or other is, without particularizing —there is in this case no one *to whom* Othello stands in the relation of believing that *she* is unfaithful, no one *of* whom he believes this, no *x* such that he believes that *x* is unfaithful. On the other hand, if we say that there is someone of whom Othello believes that she is unfaithful, while we do not thereby put *ourselves* into any relation with anyone except Othello, we do thereby say that there is someone with whom *he* stands in the relation of believing her unfaithful.

This distinction seems at first sight clear enough; but it is in fact surrounded with many obscurities. The obscurities do not concern those cases where we are *not* inclined to say that a belief, assertion, fear, etc., puts someone into relation with someone, but rather those cases where we *are* inclined to say that it does this. One of the stock examples that we may as well take from current discussion is the case of a person Tom believing that Cicero denounced Catiline. This appears to put Tom into a certain relation with Cicero, the relation of believing that he denounced Catiline. But does it? Since Cicero was the same person as Tully, it would seem that if Tom stands in any relation to Cicero he stands in that relation to Tully; but it seems perfectly possible for Tom to believe that Cicero denounced Catiline without believing that Tully did so, since Tom may not know that Cicero and Tully were one and the same individual. We are, however, inclined to say that if Tom believes *of* Cicero that he denounced Catiline, he *ipso facto* believes this of Tully; but this is to make a distinction where we suggested there is none

K

—between Tom's believing of Tully that he denounced Catiline, and his simply believing *that Tully denounced Catiline* (for he might do the former and yet not do the latter).

Another problematic case is that in which what our belief would normally be said to be 'about' is in fact non-existent. For example, suppose that Sid has been told that Walter's horse has wings, and believes this. Can this really constitute a *relation* between Sid and Walter's horse, if in fact Walter not only has no winged horse, but has no horse at all? For the matter of that, if I say that Othello believed Desdemona to be unfaithful, can this constitute a relation between me and Othello, considering that there is in fact no such person?

We may put this difficulty in another way. Genuine relations have converses, such that if A stands in any relation to B, B *ipso facto* stands in the converse relation to A—if A is to the right of B, B is *ipso facto* to the left of A, and so on. Hence if Sid, in believing that Walter's horse has wings, thereby stands in a relation to Walter's horse, Walter's horse must stand in the converse relation to Sid, presumably that of being believed by him to have wings. But how can Walter's horse do or suffer this if in fact there is just no such animal?

One simple answer to all these difficult cases would be that their logical form is not really what it appears to be, and that there is a concealed quantification which breaks these equivalences in the way that quantifications always do. If someone who is in fact called 'Tully' is believed by Tom to have denounced Catiline, *of course* it doesn't follow that Tom believes that someone called 'Tully' denounced Catiline, for the first is of the form

(1) For some $x$, $x f$'s, and Tom believes that $x g$'s,

while the second is of the form

(2) Tom believes that (for some $x$, $x f$'s and $x g$'s),

and these are no more equivalent than

(3) For some $x$, $x f$'s, and it is not the case that $x g$'s

(i.e. 'Something that $f$'s does not $g$') is equivalent to

(4) It is not the case that (for some $x$, $x f$'s and $x g$'s)

(i.e. 'Nothing that $f$'s $g$'s'). Again, if Sid believes that something is Walter's horse and has wings, of course it does not follow that something is Walter's horse and is believed by Sid to have wings, for the latter entails that Walter has a horse and the former does not.

Some solution along these lines seems to me almost certainly the correct way of handling all such puzzles, but such solutions give rise to a number of further problems. The first one is simply this: Under what conditions would there *not* be a concealed quantification in what is believed, said, feared, etc? Or in other words, under what conditions can we be sure that, in someone's belief, fear, assertion, etc., we *do* have a genuine relation between the man who believes, fears, etc., on the one hand, and an individual that his belief, fear, etc., is 'about' on the other? And if the answer to this is, as it may very well turn out to be, that *no* belief, etc., is of this simple relational form, and that there is a concealed quantification in *all* beliefs, etc., what becomes of the quite plausible distinction between 'singular' and 'general' beliefs with which we began? Can it be reinstated in some transmuted form? This is a serious question, because the expansions we have given of some of the dubious or misclassified cases of 'believing *of*' as opposed to a mere 'believing *that*', seem to assume that there are genuine cases of it. For example, if we say that 'Tom believes of Tully that he denounced Catiline' translates into 'Someone who is in fact called "Tully" is believed by Tom to have denounced Catiline', this latter suggests that there *is* someone *of* whom Tom believes that he denounced Catiline, even though Tom does not believe of this person that he is called 'Tully'. Or again, in our formal translation (1), 'For some $x$, $x f$'s, and Tom believes that $x g$'s', the last clause has the form of a relational proposition, employing the two-place predicate '— believes that — $g$'s'. If *all* beliefs contain concealed quantifications, this one needs to be still further analysed, unless there is something *like* direct reference even in some cases where there are concealed quantifications. So before falling back on so extreme a theory, we had better look at some less sceptical alternatives.

It should also be observed that even in cases where there are not merely concealed but quite overt quantifications, some curious difficulties arise. Consider, for example, the statement that the F.B.I. chief wants to catch a Communist. This may mean that there is some specific Communist that the F.B.I. chief is after, i.e. that for some $x$, $x$ is a Communist and the

F.B.I. chief wants to catch $x$. This presents no difficulties apart from the ones we have already mentioned; e.g. if the F.B.I. chief wants to catch the Communist Donaldson, and Donaldson is in fact Siskin, but the F.B.I. chief does not know this, does it follow that the F.B.I. chief wants to catch Siskin? But take it the other way; i.e. suppose the F.B.I. chief just wants to catch *a* Communist—he doesn't want his bag to be empty—though he doesn't know who the Communists are, and even if he did he wouldn't care which one he caught. (He would answer 'Yes' to 'Would you like to catch a Communist?', but have no answer at all to '*Which* Communist would you like to catch?'). In this case there is no $x$ such that $x$ is a Communist and the F.B.I. chief wants to catch $x$; it is just that the F.B.I. chief wants it to be the case that (for some $x$, $x$ is Communist, and he, the F.B.I. chief, has caught $x$). But *is* this what the F.B.I. chief wants? Our analysis of his wish amounts to this: he wants it to be the case that (someone is a Communist and is caught by him). But does a good F.B.I. chief want it to be the case that someone is a Communist? One would think not; he believes that there *are* Communists anyway, and only because there are, wants to catch one of them.

The trouble here is not due to peculiarities which wishing and wanting share with believing and saying, but rather to peculiarities which they share with *bringing something about*. This is in some ways one of the most 'extensional' of the operators we have been here considering. If one brings it about that $p$, it would seem that one *ipso facto* brings about anything that is logically equivalent to $p$; e.g. if one brings it about that all the conspirators are dead, one brings it about that none of the conspirators are not dead, and that all the French conspirators are dead and all the non-French conspirators are, and so on. But it is *not* a law in the logic of bringing-about, that if that $p$ entails that $q$ (without being entailed by it), then in bringing it about that $p$ we bring it about that $q$. For example, that someone is a Communist and is caught by the F.B.I. chief entails that someone is a Communist; but in bringing it about that (someone is a Communist and is caught by the F.B.I. chief), we do not thereby bring it about that someone is a Communist, for that may have been brought about already. Even bringing it about that all the conspirators are dead, i.e. that all the French ones and all the non-French ones are, does not entail bringing it about that all the French ones are—they may have been dead already, and the man have brought it about that *all* the conspirators are dead merely by *completing* the kill. Wanting to bring something about, and wanting something brought about, is in the like case. There is a similar peculiarity, as R. M. Chisholm has pointed out, in the logic of moral 'requirement'.[1] If certain features of a situation 'require' or 'call for' a certain response, this requirement may be cancelled or overridden by further features of the same situation; so that $p$ may require that $q$, and that $p$-and-$r$ not require that $q$, although that $p$-and-$r$ entails that $p$.

When, if ever, does a belief that $x$ $\phi$'s, or a belief that we would normally describe in that form, constitute a genuine relation between the believer and the object $x$? This is perhaps the same question as: When, if ever, is a belief that we would normally describe as belief that $x$ $\phi$'s, *really* a belief of that form, and not merely a belief that *something* $\phi$'s, or that something that $\psi$'s $\phi$'s? And this again is perhaps the same question as: When, if ever, is a belief really *about* an object $x$? The same question, or set of questions, may clearly be asked about assertions, hopes, wishes, fears, etc.

One simple answer might be that a belief that we would normally describe as a belief that $x$ $\phi$'s really is a belief of that form, and really does relate the believer to the object $x$, and really is a belief about $x$, if and only if the object $x$ actually exists. Whether the believer *knows* that $x$ exists, or whether he *believes* that $x$ exists, has on this view nothing to do with the matter. Similarly with asserting, fearing, etc.

This view, though simple, is not very plausible. Suppose, for example, that there is a person who himself holds the theory that we are considering, and who does not himself believe that Walter has a horse, but says to someone else, intending either to deceive him or to make him laugh, that Walter's horse has wings. Such a person will certainly not imagine himself to be saying *of* Walter's horse that it has wings, but merely to be pretending to do this. But if, unknown to this person, Walter really does have a horse, and exactly one horse, then the person will have said *of* this animal that it has wings, without knowing

[1] ['The Ethics of Requirement', *American Philosophical Quarterly*, 1 (1964), pp. 1–7.]

that he was doing this. Or again, suppose a person holding this theory *believes* that Walter has a horse, though he certainly doesn't *know* it, and goes on to do what he thinks is believing of Walter's horse that it has wings; then whether he really *is* doing this will depend on something of which he is totally ignorant, namely whether Walter has or has not a horse. It is not just that he is ignorant as to whether his belief that Walter's horse has wings is *true* or not; ignorance at this point is common and natural enough, but on this theory he does not even *know what he is doing* when he believes that Walter's horse has wings.

This is not a knock-down argument. We have found other reasons in an earlier chapter (about self-referential beliefs, including unconsciously self-referential ones) for holding that we do not always know what we are doing in belief-situations and in what are apparently belief-situations. But one does not want to multiply such cases unnecessarily. And in any case the suggestion only solves *one* class of difficulties, if it does that. Suppose that Walter indeed has a horse, and Sid believes that Walter's horse has wings; he may do so because he has been shown a picture of Pegasus and told that it is a picture of Walter's horse, and when shown Walter's wingless horse in a field he may say (and believe what he is saying) '*That*'s not Walter's horse— Walter's horse is the one in the picture'. Surely in this case Sid does *not* believe *of* Walter's horse that it has wings, despite the fact that he believes that Walter's horse has wings, and Walter's horse does exist.

Before dismissing this theory, however, one thing should be said: if there is such an object as *x*, and someone does something that we would normally describe as believing that *x* $\phi$'s, then the person *does* thereby put himself into *a* relation with the object *x*, even if the relation is not that of believing *of* this object that it $\phi$'s. If Sid believes that Walter's horse has wings, even if it is only because he has been shown a picture of Pegasus and told that it is Walter's horse, he does thereby stand in *a* relation to Walter's horse, if there is such an animal; for it is this animal's having wings or not which will make his belief true or false, however fantastic and misguided the grounds of the belief may be. Even if the relation between Sid and this animal is not that of believing *of* this animal that it has wings, it *is* that of having a belief which this animal's having wings would verify or falsify.

Consider another case: Suppose a certain Mrs. Murphy believes that everything that a certain Father Gordon says is true, and in particular she believes him to have spoken truly when he said that Johnny Jones had measles, although she has not the faintest idea who Johnny Jones is. If there really is a boy called Johnny Jones of whom Father Gordon said this, it is implausible under these circumstances to say that Mrs. Murphy believes *of* this boy that Father Gordon spoke truly in saying that he had measles. However, her belief puts her in *a* relation to this boy; namely that it is *his* having measles or not, and *his* having been said by Father Gordon to have them, which will make her belief true or false.

To put this in another way: Suppose that Sid's belief in the first example, and Mrs. Murphy's in the second, are essentially general in character; that is, suppose that there is no *x* such that Sid believes *of x* that it is Walter's only horse and has wings, and there is no *x* such that Mrs. Murphy believes *of x* that *x* is called Johnny Jones and has been said by Father Gordon to have measles; and that the case is merely that Sid believes *that* for some *x*, *x* is Walter's only horse and has wings, and Mrs. Murphy believes *that* for some *x*, *x* is called Johnny Jones and is said truly by Father Gordon to have measles. (We can suppose, in fact, that *whenever* the ostensible object of thought is merely believed but not known to exist, we have no more than this merely general type of belief, into which no individual as it were directly enters.) Even supposing this, however, and even in the case of such beliefs, if there is in fact such an animal as Walter's only horse, and such a boy as *the* Johnny Jones referred to by Father Gordon, then Walter's horse's having wings or not, and Johnny Jones's having been truly said or not been truly said by Father Gordon to have measles, will verify or falsify the more general propositions believed by Sid and Mrs. Murphy; and *this* will constitute *a* relation between Sid and the horse on the one hand, and Mrs. Murphy and the boy on the other.

Relations of *this* sort, however, obtain even in much vaguer cases. Suppose that the credulous Sid merely believes that *some* horses have wings, or anyhow that at least one horse has, without having any beliefs as to which horse it is that does so. Then if there is such an animal as Walter's horse, Sid stands to this animal in the relation of having a belief which this animal's having wings would verify. Indeed he stands to all horses what-ever in this relation; and for the matter of that he stands to any *object* whatever in the relation of having a belief which would be true if this object had wings and were a horse. So not too much, perhaps, should be made of this concession; we may find it useful, all the same, later on.

In considering theories about when belief consists in a relation between the believer and an object that the belief is about, it is always necessary to consider how the theory works out with beliefs that are ostensibly about the beliefs of other people, or beliefs that are ostensibly about the statements or fears of other people, or fears or statements that are ostensibly about the beliefs of other people, and so on. The example about Mrs. Murphy is already of this character, and is therefore worth looking at more closely from this point of view. The ostensible relation involved in Mrs. Murphy's belief that Father Gordon has said truly that Johnny Jones has measles is a triadic one. On the theory that we are now considering the belief will actually constitute such a relation if and only if all three terms (i.e. Mrs. Murphy, Father Gordon, and Johnny Jones) actually exist; in any case, there is at least *a* relation between these terms (to do with the verification or falsification of Mrs. Murphy's belief and Father Gordon's statement) if all three of them exist. If, on the other hand, Father Gordon exists but Johnny Jones does not, Mrs. Murphy's belief will indeed relate her to Father Gordon, but not to Johnny Jones; she will in this case genuinely believe *of* Father Gordon that he has said *that* Johnny Jones has measles, and she will believe *that* Johnny Jones actually *has* measles, though how the name 'Johnny Jones' enters into these descriptions of her belief is left obscure.

What is also obscure, in this case, is whether Mrs. Murphy is able to *believe of* Father Gordon that he has said *of* Johnny Jones that he has measles; though it is clear that he cannot on this theory have *really* said this *of* Johnny Jones, so that if Mrs. Murphy *could* have such a belief it would be a mistaken one, and moreover would not itself be a believing *of* Johnny Jones that something-or-other, e.g. that he had been said by Father Gor-don to have measles. That is, the theory as stated is quite definite that X cannot believe anything *of* Z unless Z exists, but it leaves open the question whether X can believe of an existing

Y that Y believes or says something *of* a Z which in fact doesn't exist. A single 'of' entails existence; but does an 'of' within the scope of another 'of' entail existence also? No doubt the theory is capable of further development in either direction; but if the use of a second-order 'of' does *not* entail existence, then for *internal* beliefs or statements some other theory will need to be developed, and in that case we might just as well have had this theory for the outermost ones too.

# 10

## RUSSELLIAN NAMES AND DESCRIPTIONS

THE second theory that I wish to consider, about the conditions under which a belief can constitute a relation between a believer and an object that the belief is about, is the theory that this can occur only if the believer knows, beyond any possibility of mistake, that the object in question exists. It is perhaps easier to consider this type of theory, to begin with, in connection with saying rather than believing. The corresponding theory about saying would be broadly that X is able to say something *of* Y if he is in a position to refer to Y by means of a 'logically proper name' in Russell's sense; or that when X says that Y $\phi$'s, this constitutes a genuine relation between X and Y if and only if in saying that Y $\phi$'s, X refers to Y by means of a Russellian proper name.

Russell's theory of proper names is a descendant of John Stuart Mill's. Mill, in his *System of Logic*, divides names into 'singular' and 'general', and then into 'connotative' and 'non-connotative'. Mill's 'general names' are, by and large, common nouns and adjectives, and all of these are, in his sense, 'connotative'. He does not consider *enumerations* of objects, but if he had considered them, might possibly have classified them as general but non-connotative. But ordinary general names such as 'man' or 'horse' (or 'white') are in his sense connotative. The objects to which these words in fact apply (or which, as he rather unhappily puts it, they 'denote') do not constitute any part of their meaning. We can in principle understand them without knowing what objects they apply to, though perhaps this needs to be qualified in the case of simple general terms like 'red', of which it is arguable that we can only learn their meaning by seeing actual things of the sort in question. Even in these cases, however, the meaning of the word is not altered by its coming to apply to different objects. Moreover, a common noun or adjective still means whatever it does mean even if it applies to no objects at all. They apply to objects as being of certain sorts, or as Mill puts it, as possessing certain attributes; to understand such a word, we must understand what attributes a thing must have for the word to apply to it. The attributes which thus fix the meaning of a common noun or adjective are said by Mill to be 'connoted' by it.

When we come to consider singular terms, these may or may not be connotative. Some singular terms are formed by attaching some individualizing prefix such as 'the' or 'this' to a connotative expression, as in 'the present Prime Minister of England'; such expressions we can understand without knowing what objects they apply to, and indeed without knowing whether they apply to any; and they apply to objects, when they do, as the unique possessors of some attribute or attributes, which attributes they are therefore said to 'connote'. With *proper* names, however, the case is different. A proper name, Mill sometimes says, is a 'meaningless mark'. Its sole function is to identify the object we are talking about, not to convey any information about this object. We may in fact *have* a certain amount of previous information about the object denoted by a proper name, and the name may call this to mind, but that is no part of its actual use in a sentence, and no part of its meaning.

The Platonistic suggestions of Mill's constant use of the term 'attributes' are not essential to the theory. Much more important is his talk of connotative terms as 'conveying information'. What he was getting at was rather close to the suggestion later made explicitly by C. S. Peirce, that common nouns and adjectives are dispensable parts of speech, and all that they do can be done less misleadingly by verbs. What common nouns, adjectives, and verbs all have in common is that they do not directly *name* objects, but may nevertheless *apply* to objects. The common noun 'chair' applies to an object *x* if *x is a chair*; the adjective 'white' applies to an object *x* if *x is white*; and the verb 'smokes' applies to an object *x* if *x smokes*. The italicized expressions, it will be noticed, when taken as a whole, all have the force of verbs, and when we use common nouns or adjectives they always occur either implicitly or explicitly as parts of such verbs. When a common noun is used as a subject-term, as in 'Every man is running', 'man' does not occur explicitly as part of the verb 'is a man', but this verb is nevertheless implicitly present, since the whole is equivalent to 'Whatever is a man is running'. Similarly, when an adjective directly qualifies a noun, as in 'X is a bad man', 'bad' does not occur explicitly as part of the verb 'is bad', but this verb is implicitly present, since the whole is equivalent to 'X is bad and is a man'. 'Connotative names', one might say, simply are not names at all, but are 'predicative' in force.

That this was the general drift of Mill's remarks on this subject is clear from the use that he makes of his basic distinctions in later parts of his *System*. In discussing 'the import of propositions', he considers separately the case in which the subject is non-connotative and the predicate is connotative, as in 'Chimborazo is white', and the case in which both terms are connotative, as in 'All men are mortal'. In the former case, the meaning is 'that the individual thing denoted by the subject, has the attributes connoted by the predicate'; in the latter that 'whatever has the attributes connoted by the subject, has also those connoted by the predicate', e.g. 'Whatever has the attributes of man has the attributes of mortality'. The important point is that in both cases the analysis gets the connotative term into a predicative position.

Proper names, on the other hand, do not, or anyhow need not, function as parts of verbs or predicates. At least, this was Mill's original doctrine; Peirce modified it. For Peirce, what was important was the distinction between the 'diagrammatic' and the 'indexical'. He wrote:

Diagrams and diagrammatoidal figures are intended to be applied to the better understanding of states of things. . . . Such a figure cannot, however, show what it is to which it is intended to be applied; nor can any other diagram avail for that purpose. The where and the when of the particular experience . . . to which the diagram is to be applied, are things not capable of being diagrammatically exhibited. Describe and describe and describe, and you never can describe a date, a position, or any homaloidal quantity. You may object that a map is a diagram showing localities; undoubtedly, but not until the law of the projection is understood, and not even then unless at least two points on the map are somehow previously identified with points in nature. Now, how is any diagram ever to perform that identification? If a diagram cannot do it, algebra cannot: for algebra is but a sort of diagram; and if algebra cannot do it, language cannot: for language is but a kind of algebra. It would, certainly, in one sense be extravagant to say that we can never tell what we are talking about; yet, in another sense, it is quite true.[1]

The only remedy for this defect of 'language' is to have expressions in it which are in a sense only half-linguistic, their function being as it were to drag some bit of the world right into what is being said. Leading us to this, Peirce goes on:

That the diagrammatisation is one thing and the application of the diagram quite another, is recognised obscurely in the structure of such languages as I am acquainted with, which distinguishes the *subjects* and *predicates* of propositions. The subjects are the indications of the things spoken of, the predicates, the words that assert, question or command whatever is intended. Only, the shallowness of syntax is manifest in its failing to recognise the impotence of mere words, and especially of common nouns, to fulfil the function of a grammatical subject. Words like *this, that, lo, hallo, hi there,* have a direct, forceful action upon the nervous system, and compel the hearer to look about him; and so they, more than ordinary words, contribute towards indicating what the speech is about. But this is a point that grammar and the grammarians . . . are so far from seeing as to call demonstratives, such as *that* and *this*, pronouns—a literally preposterous designation, for nouns may more truly be called prodemonstratives.[2]

Even proper nouns; though Peirce is a little inconstant here. 'Every language', he says in one place, 'must have proper names; and there is no verb wrapped up in a proper name.'[3] This makes them pure 'indices', but he goes on to say that this is true of a proper name only 'when one meets with it for the first time', when it 'is existentially connected with some percept or other equivalent individual knowledge of the individual it names'. After that, it is merely 'an Icon of that Index' (2. 329), i.e. it is a replica of the sound we heard when introduced to its bearer; it means, in effect, 'he to whom we were introduced as N.M.'. Of proper names (e.g. 'Caesar') which we learn to apply not in this but in other ways, Peirce here says nothing, but there is no

---

[1] [*Collected Papers*, 3, p. 419.]    [2] [Ibid.]    [3] [Ibid. 2, p. 328.]

reason to suppose that he would dissent from Russell's view of them as 'disguised descriptions'.

Russell's main contribution to this line of thought is his fairly simple analysis of what Mill called singular connotative names, at least of those of the form 'The $\phi$-er', or 'The thing that $\phi$'s', or more exactly 'The only thing that $\phi$'s'. In effect, as Geach has pointed out, this analysis has two parts. The explicitly predicative use of such phrases, i.e. its use within the form '$x$ is the only thing that $\phi$'s', is analysed as '$x$ $\phi$'s, and nothing else $\phi$'s', or in full '$x$ $\phi$'s, and whatever $\phi$'s is identical with $x$', or 'Anything $\phi$'s if and only if it is identical with $x$'. The use of the phrase as an ostensible subject is then explained by explicating an implicitly predicative use. In principle this could be done in either of two ways; that is, we could expand 'The only thing that $\phi$'s, $\psi$'s' either as 'Something at once is-the-only-thing-that-$\phi$'s, and $\psi$'s' or as 'If anything is-the-only-thing-that-$\phi$'s, it $\psi$'s'. The former is automatically false, and the latter automatically true, if nothing is-the-only-thing-that-$\phi$'s, i.e. if either nothing $\phi$'s or more than one thing $\phi$'s. Russell chooses the first alternative.

One consequence of this analysis is that there is no difficulty about saying that the $\phi$-er, i.e. the only thing that $\phi$'s, exists, and that it doesn't exist, and either of these may be true in a given case. 'The $\phi$-er exists', or 'There is such a thing as the $\phi$-er', means simply that something is the only thing that $\phi$'s, and 'The $\phi$-er does not exist', or 'There is no such thing as the $\phi$-er', means simply that nothing is the only thing that $\phi$'s.

Another consequence of the Russellian analysis of these phrases is that a difference has to be made between using the phrase 'the $\phi$-er' as the subject of a complex predicate in a simple sentence, and using it within an analogously complex sentence. For example, 'The $\phi$-er (does not $\psi$)' has a different analysis from 'It is not the case that (the $\phi$-er $\psi$'s)', since the former means 'Something both is-the-only-thing-that-$\phi$'s, and does not $\psi$', while the latter means 'It is not the case that (something both is-the-only-thing-that-$\phi$'s, and $\psi$'s)'. Again, 'The $\phi$-er (is said to $\psi$)' differs from 'It is said that (the $\phi$-er $\psi$'s)'; the former means that something both is-the-only-thing-that-$\phi$'s and is-said-to-$\psi$, and the latter that it is said that (something both is-the-only-thing-that $\phi$'s, and $\psi$'s). This is simply a special case of the difference we have already noticed between a 'something' that stands outside and one that stands inside some other operator.

What Russell means by a logically proper name is best seen by contrasting it at these two points with what he calls a definite description, i.e. an expression of the form 'the only thing that $\phi$'s'. In the first place, it is not possible with a logically proper name '$x$' to form or interpret the sentences '$x$ exists' and '$x$ doesn't exist'. At least, this is how Russell puts it, but as Moore has pointed out, his view here can easily be modified without affecting his general position. The point is that if a logically proper name fails to denote any object, it loses every vestige of meaning that it has, since it has, as Peirce put it, no verb wrapped up in it to carry any further meaning. This means that where '$x$' is a logically proper name, and actually functions in forming meaningful sentences, it must denote an object, and '$x$ exists' is bound to be true and '$x$ does not exist' false. This still distinguishes it sharply from definite descriptions; 'The $\phi$-er exists' *can* be false, and 'The $\phi$-er does not exist' *can* be true.

A logically proper name also differs from a definite description in that the attachment of a complex predicate to it *does* mean exactly the same as its occurrence in the corresponding complex sentence. Where '$x$' is a logically proper name, '$x$ is not red' means no more and no less than 'It is not the case that $x$ is red', and '$x$ is said by Y to be red' means no more and no less than 'Y says that $x$ is red'. In fact, in a language containing logically proper names, complex predicates are simply not required. Their elimination from sentences which themselves contain logically proper names has just been illustrated; their eliminability from sentences containing definite descriptions follows from Russell's analysis of such sentences, coupled with the understanding that bound individual variables stand for logically proper names. For example, 'The $\phi$-er is a non-$\psi$-er', or 'The $\phi$-er does-not-$\psi$', amounts to 'For some $x$, (1) $x$ $\phi$'s, (2) nothing other than $x$ $\phi$'s, and (3) it is not the case that $x$ $\psi$'s'. In the last conjunct, it will be observed, the complexity of the predicate 'does not $\psi$', has been replaced by the use of the analogously complex sentence.

We might use just these features to *define* the concept of a Russellian name; or we might use them to define the concept of *using* a given expression *as* a Russellian name. We might say, for instance, that an expression $N$ is being used as a Russellian name only if there is an object $x$ such that $\ulcorner\phi N\urcorner$ means precisely that $x$ $\phi$'s, and means nothing else; and if there is no such object $x$, $\ulcorner\phi N\urcorner$ is simply ill formed, or at all events is without any truth-value. Further, expressions $N$ and $M$ are being used as logically proper names only if *any* sentences in which they are both used (we exclude sentences in which they are merely mentioned) express *relations* between the objects with which they are correlated as in the preceding stipulation, which relations have converses obeying the usual rules, in particular, where $\phi$ and $\psi$ are converses, $\ulcorner\phi MN\urcorner$ and $\ulcorner\psi NM\urcorner$ are logically equivalent. Again, an expression $N$ is being used as a Russellian name only if, where $\delta$ is any expression that forms sentences from sentences and predicates from predicates, e.g. 'not', 'allegedly', or 'possibly', $\ulcorner(\delta\phi)N\urcorner$ is indistinguishable in sense from $\ulcorner\delta(\phi N)\urcorner$.

I suspect that this last criterion amounts to saying that Russellian names always figure as *arguments* of proposition-forming functions and never as functions of those functions.[1] Roughly: a context of a context of a genuine 'argument' $x$ is a context of $x$; and this will hold for intentional contexts of contexts also. 'I think that this is a man' is synonymous with 'This is thought by me to be a man', when '— is a man' is a genuine context of the argument 'this' and 'I think that —' a genuine context of this context.

This free handling of contexts of contexts as contexts is not possible, however, if we obstinately treat as an argument-in-a-context what is really a context of that context. For example, if in 'Every animal is not a man' we treat 'is not a man' as a function attached to 'Every animal' as its argument rather than vice versa. So interpreted, the sentence will express the false proposition that all animals are non-human, and it will express this by putting the subject 'every animal' into the complex context '— is not a man'; but the simple '— is a man' (out of which the preceding is constructed by adding 'not') is not a context of this subject at all; if we attached '— is a man' to 'Every animal' and then used 'not' to negate the whole thus formed, what would be expressed would be the quite different

---

[1] [At this point, in accordance with a note of Prior's, we have inserted a passage from his paper 'Is the Concept of Referential Opacity Really Necessary?', *Acta sophica Fennica*, 16 (1963), 196–8.]

(and true) proposition that not all animals are men. If, however, we rewrite the sentence (retaining the meaning indicated) in a structure-indicating pidgin as '(Every animal (not (is a man)))', where the verb 'is a man' is treated as the argument, it becomes a matter of indifference whether we think of this verb as formed into a negative verb by adding the inner context or function 'not', and the result formed into a sentence by adding the outer context or functor 'Every animal', or whether we think of this outer function as being first applied to 'not' to give the more complex sentence-forming function of verbs '(Every animal (not (. . .)))'—abbreviable to '(No animal (. . .))'—which is then applied to 'is a man' to give the same ultimate result.

There are, notoriously, similar cases where the applicative 'every' is replaced by 'the' and the truth-functional adverb 'not' by non-extensional ones like 'possibly', 'allegedly'; and they are to be dealt with along the same lines. For instance: 'The Morning Star has been denied to be the Morning Star', which we may consider to be true because someone who has seen Venus in the evening and not known it to be the Morning Star has denied it to be so. Here, it might be said, the complex context 'has been denied to be the Morning Star' is wrapped around 'The Morning Star' as the sentence's logical subject; but then it would have to be admitted that the simpler predicate 'is the Morning Star', out of which the other is constructed, is not a context of this subject; if we attached 'is the Morning Star' to 'The Morning Star' and then used 'It has been denied that' to form a wider whole, what would be expressed would be not what has been given but the false proposition that it has been denied that the Morning Star is the Morning Star. If we rewrite the whole as '(Something that is the only Morning Star (allegedly not (is the Morning Star)))' we have no such trouble, for it is a matter of indifference whether this be thought of as the result of first using 'allegedly not' to construct the complex verb 'allegedly not (is the Morning Star)' (i.e. 'has been denied to be the Morning Star') out of the simpler 'is the Morning Star', and then using the prefix 'Something, etc.' to build up the whole from this, or whether we think of it as formed by first applying that prefix to 'allegedly not' to construct the more complex prefix 'Something, etc. (allegedly not. . .)', and then applying this to 'is the Morning Star' to form the same whole. And note that this remedy does not consist in regarding the context 'has been denied to be the Morning Star' as a peculiar sort of context requiring special treatment, but to deny that *either* 'has been denied to be the Morning Star' *or* the simple (and extensional) 'is the Morning Star' are 'contexts' of 'The Morning Star' at all—the context-subject relation rather runs, in this case, the other way.[1]

Well, where what we attach to the verb is a Russellian name, the context-subject relation doesn't run the other way, but runs from the verb to the noun. If we *do* use features like this for a definition of a Russellian name, or of using an expression as a Russellian name, we may find this concept exemplified in unexpected ways. For example, it may be that phrases of the form 'The $\phi$-er' can be used as Russellian names as well as having the quite different use that Russell assigns to them. We may, for example, so use the phrase 'The man over there', in a sentence like 'The man over there is clever', that its sole purpose is to identify the individual of whom we wish to say that he is clever, and the sentence may be being used simply to say that that particular individual is clever, and not at all to say, for example, that the individual is a man, or that he is 'over there'. The sentence used would then be true if and only if the individual meant *was* clever, and it would still be true if it turned out that the individual was not a man but a woman or a Robot, or that he had moved into a different position without our noticing it. And with the phrase being thus used, 'I think that the man over there is clever' *would* be precisely equivalent to 'The man over there is thought by me to be clever'; both would mean that I ascribe cleverness to a certain individual, and would be true if and only if I did so. Where the phrase is used as a Russellian description, the case is of course different. To say that I think there is someone who is a man and is the only man in a certain corner and is clever, is *not* the same as to say that there *is* someone who is a man and is the only man in that corner and is thought by me to be clever; the latter would have to be false, though the former could be true, if there were no men in the corner, or several. And if phrases of the form 'the $\phi$-er' can be used as Russellian names, no doubt ordinary proper names can be so used also. We might use 'Johnny Jones' in 'Johnny Jones has measles' simply to identify a certain individual and say of

[1] [The insertion ends at this point.]

him that he had measles, so that this would be true if this individual had measles, even if for example, his name were not really 'Johnny Jones'.

In belief-contexts, what all this means is that if 'X' and 'Y' are both Russellian logically proper names, 'Y is believed by X to $\phi$', e.g. to have denounced Catiline, means no more and no less than 'X believes that Y $\phi$'s', and either form expresses a genuine relation between X and Y. Again if 'X', 'Y', and 'Z' are all three of them logically proper names, the following forms are all equivalent: 'X believes that Y says that Z $\phi$'s', 'Y is believed by X to say that Z $\phi$'s', 'X believes that Z is said by Y to $\phi$', and 'Z is believed by X to be said by Y to $\phi$'. This is, as far as it goes, a very pleasant consequence, provided that there *can* be expressions which function in the way that logically proper names are said to do. But much that Peirce says, and much that Russell says also, would suggest that it is only comparatively rarely that we are in a position to use logically proper names at all, and that in at least many cases one person will be in a position to use such names and another person not. This has the consequence that often all that is possible for one person is to give a comparatively general account, or to have comparatively general opinions, of what another person says or believes; so that Y may say or believe something and X be quite unable to say or have an opinion about *exactly* what it is that Y says or believes. For Y may be in a position to say *of* Z that he $\phi$'s, e.g. by using the sentence 'This man $\phi$'s', and X *not* be in a position to say *of* Z that Y says that he $\phi$'s, but only in a position to say that for *some* unique $w$, perhaps for some unique $w$ that is called 'Z', Y says that $w$ $\phi$'s. Similarly with beliefs. At the same time X *can* distinguish, both out loud and in thought, between there being something *of* which Y says or believes that it $\phi$'s, and Y's merely saying or believing *that something $\phi$'s*.

On the other hand, we might find that with this definition of a Russellian name, there are no Russellian names at all, or that the specified use of expressions is impossible, e.g. that there is no form of words by which we can *just* say of a certain individual that he has measles, and *mean* that and nothing else. What is it to *mean that* a certain individual has measles, and mean nothing else? Is this, for example, something we can conceivably do without knowing we are doing it, or that we can think we are doing without really doing it? If so, and if we do on occasion think we are meaning that a certain individual has measles when in fact we are not doing so, what would this *thinking that we mean that thing* consist in? How can we identify the thing that we think we mean, even in order to think we mean it, except by thinking something directly *of* a certain individual, namely that we think we mean that he has measles; and if we *can* do this, what on earth could *stop* us from *really* meaning that he has measles? But if, when we thus mean that a certain individual has measles, we cannot be mistaken as to which individual we mean has measles, and certainly cannot think that there is an individual of whom we mean this when there is none, this infallible connection between us and that individual cannot be one that obtains very often or very easily (indeed Russell himself insists that this is so); and it will at least very often be the case that when we are in a position to say something which means that a certain individual has measles, and means nothing else, other people will *not* be in a position to say anything that means that this same individual is said by us to have measles, and means nothing else but that.

# APPENDIX

## NAMES

BY a *name* logicians generally understand an expression that we use to indicate *which* individual we are talking about when we are making a statement. And some logicians, Russell in particular, seem to take the view that when we make statements in which we refer to an individual by name, the making of such a statement constitutes an actual *relation* between the speakers and the individual in question, so that where 'Y' is a Russellian name, the following forms are logically equivalent:

(A) X says that Y is bald
(B) X says of Y that he is bald
(C) Y is said by X to be bald.

And the problem about this use of the term 'name' is simply this: What expressions, if any, *are* names in this sense? In looking at examples, I don't think we need give any further thought to case (C) as distinct from (B), as cases (B) and (C) seem equivalent *whatever* we put for Y. But, concentrating on (A) and (B), it is easy to find cases which do *not* fill the bill, and which in fact no one would count as names. For example, the following are clearly *not* equivalent:

(1) X says that *no one* is bald
(2) X says of *no one* that he is bald (i.e. X does not say of anyone that he is).

Similarly these are not equivalent:

(3) X says that *someone* is bald
(4) X says of *someone* that *he* is bald.

Nor are these:

(5) X says that *the present King of France* is bald.
(6) X says of *the present King of France* that he is bald.

Here (5) might be true but (6) cannot be true because there is no present King of France. But neither are these equivalent:

(7) X says that *the present King of Sweden* is bald
(8) X says of *the present King of Sweden* that he is bald.

For X might meet the present King of Sweden, and say in his presence 'This man is bald', which would be to say of the present King of Sweden that he is bald, but would not be to say *that* the present King of Sweden is bald. These well-known facts have led Russell to assimilate cases (5)–(8) to cases (1) and (2) by reading (7) and (8), say, as

> (9) X says that there is someone who is the sole present King of Sweden and who is bald.
> (10) Someone is the sole present King of Sweden and X says of him that he is bald.

But even the following, notoriously, are not equivalent:

> (11) X says that Sherlock Holmes is bald
> (12) X says of Sherlock Holmes that he is bald,

(12) being ruled out for the same reason as (6). And even these are at least questionable:

> (13) X says that Winston Churchill is bald
> (14) X says of Winston Churchill that he is bald.

For if X meets Winston Churchill, not knowing him to be Winston Churchill, and perhaps even believing him not to be Winston Churchill, and says 'This man is bald', he will have said of Winston Churchill that he is bald, but it is doubtful whether he will have said *that Winston Churchill is bald*. And *these* well-known facts have led Russell to assimilate cases (11) to (14), despite the fact that both 'Sherlock Holmes' and 'Winston Churchill' *would* ordinarily be counted as names, to cases (5) to (8); i.e. he assimilates grammatical proper names to expressions of the form 'The so-and-so', which he calls 'definite descriptions'. Just how this is to be done in each particular case is left to the imagination.

What expressions *do* meet the Russellian requirements? Russell's own view is that they are generally met by *demonstratives*, with of course appropriate accompanying gestures. So let's look now at

> (15) X says that *this* individual is bald
> (16) X says of *this* individual that he is bald.

It must be admitted that these *do* seem to be logically equivalent— it's very hard to conceive conditions which would verify either of them without *ipso facto* verifying the other. What seems to disappear when we come to *these* examples is a certain gap between X's own point of view and the point of view of his reporter. If you look back at all the previous pairs you will notice that they all have the following features:

(*a*) With the *first* member of each pair, the reporter tells us *exactly* what X says, and tells us this is what would probably be X's own words; e.g. in the first example, the reporter tells us that X says *that no one is bald*, and we are to take it that this is *exactly* what X said, and that he either said it by uttering this very sentence 'No one is bald', or by uttering one entirely synonymous with it. And so on with all the examples right down to 'X says that Winston Churchill is bald', and it is of course the same with example (15).

(*b*) But with the *second* member of each pair, in all the *previous* examples, i.e. in all the examples *except* (16), the reporter *doesn't* tell us *exactly* what X says, but only tells us the *kind* of statement that X makes, leaving it to X to fill in the details. By and large the reporter, in the earlier cases, leaves it to X to identify the individual he is talking about, and doesn't, in reporting X's statement, himself talk about the individual in the same direct way that X does. This contrast of course is worked out a bit differently in different cases. Example (2) about 'no one' is a sort of zero case that hardly fits the description I've just given; we'll let it be. In case (4), about 'someone' the reporter's point of view differs from X's *exactly* as I have said—the reporter in no sense tells us *which* individual it is that X says is bald; he leaves that to X entirely. In at least some of the cases involving definite descriptions and proper names, there are no doubt senses in which the reporter *does* say which individual it is that X says is bald; but he doesn't, or anyhow doesn't necessarily, identify the individual exactly as X does, and in general does so less directly. But in example (16) the reporter says *which* individual it is at least as explicitly as X says it, and, to that extent at least, tells us *exactly* what it is that X says, in what may be presumed to be X's own words, and so the difference from (15) vanishes.

(*c*) In all the other examples, in the *first* member of each pair, the reporter is able to tell us exactly what X says without himself being committed to any beliefs of an existential sort—he can tell us that X says that someone is bald, or that the King of France or the King of Sweden or Holmes or Churchill is, without himself being committed to any beliefs in the existence of any of these persons. And in the *second* member of each pair, the reporter's commitments seem to be different from X's commitments, and the reporter doesn't in fact tell us what X's commitments are. The man who says, e.g., that X says of Sherlock Holmes that he is bald, implies that he himself believes in the existence of Sherlock Holmes, but not that X does—for all that the report tells us, X might say of Sherlock Holmes that he is bald without realizing that it is Holmes of whom he says it. But with (15) and (16) all this changes. The reporter cannot say that X says that *this* individual is bald without himself identifying the individual and being as much committed to his existence as X is.

What these contrasts suggest is that in (15) and (16) the web of language is somehow broken through and X and the reporter have both put their hand on a bit of reality, and the same bit of reality. And that, I think, is just what is supposed to happen with a Russellian name. But does it? I'm not sure. And *one* reason why I'm not sure is that (15) and (16) retain their peculiarities when the *'this'* which occurs in them is not demonstrative at all, but relative. That is, (15) and (16) *stay* equivalent when they occur not in isolation, or just eked out by gestures, but when they occur as part of a *story*, as in (17) and (18):

> (17) There lives in Baker Street an individual who is called 'Sherlock Holmes', is a detective, plays the violin, takes cocaine, etc.; and X says that this individual is bald.
> (18) There lives in Baker Street an individual who is called 'Sherlock Holmes', is a detective, plays the violin, takes cocaine, etc.; and X says of this individual that he is bald.

That is, we imagine some such story as this: 'There lives in Baker Street an individual named "Sherlock Holmes", and this individual is a detective, uses cocaine, etc.', and then it makes no odds whether we finish up with 'and X says that this individual is bald' or with 'X says of this individual that he is bald'. Either way the individual is identified not by his place in X's story but by his place in the reporter's story; and if you want to do it the other way you have to use not (17) or (18) but (19),

> (19) X says that there lives in Baker Street an individual who is called 'Sherlock Holmes', is a detective, etc., and X says that this individual is bald (or says of this individual that he is bald)

in which it's explicitly said that it's *X* that starts the story that there lives an individual in Baker Street, etc. The natural way to finish *this* case—in which it's explicitly X's story that the individual figures in—is by saying 'and X says that this individual is bald'. But if one did finish it 'and X says of this individual that he is bald', or even 'and this individual is said by X to be bald', wouldn't it be natural to understand *these* versions too as being about an individual in X's story?

At all events it is clear that where a background story is involved, the important thing is whether it's X's story or the reporter's own, and this can always be explicitly indicated. Moreover, exactly this question—who is telling the background story—is important, at least when there *is* a background story, when we are using ordinary proper names.

Look at (17), (18), and (19) again, and for 'this individual' just put 'Sherlock Holmes'. Once again the difference will be not between (17) and (18) but between (17) and (19).

And in the case of ordinary proper names, isn't there *always* a background story involved? Certainly there has to be in a case like Sherlock Holmes, but even in the case of Churchill—well, how many of us have met or even seen Churchill? And even if we have, what does this mean except that our background story includes a bit that goes '. . . and this individual was introduced to us as "Churchill" . . .'. Perhaps there's always a background story even with demonstratives —a story of the form 'There's an individual I am pointing to, and . . .' or it may be 'There's an individual X is pointing to, and . . .'—and these make a difference to (15) and (16). (9) and (10) in fact give the underlying pattern not only of the items that precede them but also of the items that come after them.

Now *that*'s all by way of preliminary—I don't think it's very discussable, but it's an essential prelude to a question that I think is discussable, and that is the question as to what each of these numbered statements is *about*. There's a close connection between the concept of a name and the concept of being about something. Prima facie, when a name occurs in a sentence, the name names an individual that the sentence is about. But many logicians make a sharp distinction between this pair of concepts and another pair. Some expressions, it is said, *name* or *refer to* individuals, while others merely *apply* to them. A verb such as 'smokes' applies to an individual Y if Y smokes, but no one would say in these circumstances that the verb *names* Y. An adjective such as 'bald' applies to an individual Y if Y is bald, but no one would say in these circumstances that 'bald' *names* Y. And a common noun such as 'man' or 'King of Sweden' *applies* to Y if Y is a man or is a King of Sweden, but it wouldn't generally be said that 'man' or 'King of Sweden' names or is the name of Y in this case. And the same is often said of singular descriptions. Descriptions like 'the present King of Sweden' don't *name* anyone, but there is someone—Gustav VI—that this description *applies to*. And the difference between applying to and naming is sometimes said to be that what an expression *applies to* is no part of its meaning—we can understand a sentence in which a description occurs without knowing who the description applies to, and we could understand it, and would understand it in the same way, even if the description happened to apply to no one at all—but the whole meaning of a genuine name is the individual that it identifies or indicates; or if you don't like that language, the whole contribution which a genuine name makes to the meaning of a sentence is its indication or identification of an individual. And in the case of a sentence containing a name, what the sentence is about is part of the sentence's meaning; but where the sentence only contains a description, what the description applies to is no part of the sentence's meaning, no part of what is said, though a sentence like 'The present King of Sweden is bald' may be *verified* by the circumstance that Gustav VI is bald. We might coin the expression 'verifier' here and say that Gustav is the verifier of this statement. We could say if we like that this sentence is *indirectly about* Gustav, but not *directly about* him, it being understood that what a sentence is directly about enters into its very meaning, whereas what it is *indirectly about* does not. Whether a sentence is directly about anything depends on the *form* of the sentence, and in particular on whether it does or does not contain a genuine name, while whether it is indirectly about anything depends not on its form but on a fact of nature. 'The King of France is bald' and 'The King of Sweden is bald' are neither of them directly about anything, because neither of them contains a genuine name—neither of them is of the right form—but it happens, as a matter of historical fact, that 'The King of France is bald' isn't indirectly about anything either, whereas 'The King of Sweden is bald' *is* indirectly about Gustav VI.

Note, however, that if we accept *this* whole story, we are again led to the conclusion that ordinary proper names aren't genuine names in the sense that fits the story, and that if there *are* any genuine names in the sense that fits the story they will be demonstratives. For 'Sherlock Holmes is bald' isn't directly about any individual whatever, and if it depends on a proposition's *form* whether it's directly about anything or not, 'Winston Churchill is bald' isn't directly about anything either, since that is of the *same* form as 'Sherlock Holmes is bald', though we can still contrast the two cases on the side of what they are *indirectly* about—'Holmes is bald' isn't even indirectly about anything, but 'Churchill is bald' is indirectly about Churchill. So it looks as if none of our propositions except (15) and (16) is directly about anything—unless of course they're all directly about X. On the other hand, the second member of each pair (apart from (2)) seems to imply that X says something directly about Y, at all events if we read 'says *of* Y' as 'says directly about Y', and what seems to distinguish (15) and (16) from the rest is that in these ones the reporter also speaks directly about Y. So if there's no such thing as direct aboutness, the distinctions drawn in the earlier pairs, which certainly seem to represent real distinctions, must be otherwise accounted for. Perhaps they can be. For the second member of each pair *implies* that there is something that X speaks about at best *in*directly, i.e. implies that the term Y, whatever it is, applies to something, while the first member of each pair doesn't have this implication. That is, we *could* read 'says of' as 'says *in*directly about', and still preserve these distinctions.

I ought in conclusion to mention one view about names which

is fairly popular nowadays but which I don't think is tenable. This is the view that a name is any logically simple expression by which a person *intends* to identify an actual object, whether he succeeds in actually doing so or not. This raises what seem to me insuperable difficulties when names occur in indirect speech, as in our example (11)—'X says that Sherlock Holmes is bald'. Suppose that X believes that there is such a person as Holmes but the reporter does not. Then X is in a position to be using 'Holmes' as a name, and is presumably doing so, i.e. he intends to refer to this supposed person by it, but the reporter cannot have any such intention, and therefore cannot use 'Holmes' as a name, and so cannot be reporting exactly what X is saying. The only way out of this is *either* to say that an expression is only a genuine name if the intention to refer cannot by the very nature of the case be frustrated, so that in the case of 'Sherlock Holmes' neither the reporter *nor* X himself uses it as a genuine name; *or* to say that a name is still a name, is still being used in the same way and used to make the same statement, whether it has application or not, and whether it is known to have application or not.[1]

*Principia Mathematica* contains a theorem, namely *24.52, which asserts that the universal class is not empty, that is, that there is at least one individual. And this is a theorem which Russell found an embarrassment—in a footnote to his *Introduction to Mathematical Philosophy* (p. 203) he describes it as 'a defect in logical purity'. In Leśniewski's ontology this defect, if it is one, doesn't exist—ontology is compatible with an empty universe. What is puzzling is the explanation which is commonly given of this achievement. The lowest-type variables of ontology are described, like Russell's lowest-type variables, as standing for *names*; but it is said that whereas Russell's variables stand for singular names only, Leśniewski's stand equally for empty names, singular names and plural names. Existence is therefore something that can be significantly predicated with an ontological 'name' as subject—'*a* exists' is a well-formed formula, and is in some cases but not in all cases true, and that it is true in some cases is, although true and statable, not a theorem of the system. Another peculiarity, connected with the preceding ones, is that the ontological symbol 'ε', unlike the Russellian symbol 'ε', stands between expressions of the same logical type. '*a* ε *a*', for example, is well-formed.

---

[1] [The next ten paragraphs are taken from a paper 'Existence in Leśniewski and in Russell', printed in *Formal Systems and Recursive Functions*, ed. J. M. Crossley and M. A. E. Dummett, pp. 149–55. This appeared to us suitable to fill a lacuna in the MS of 'Names' which was clearly meant to be filled with a discussion of Leśniewski's Ontology.]

What are we to make of all this? I want to suggest that what we are to make of it is that ontology is just a broadly Russellian theory of classes deprived of any variables of Russell's lowest logical type. Ontology's so-called 'names', in other words, are not individual names in the Russellian sense, but *class* names. This immediately explains the first two of the peculiarities I have mentioned. For while it makes nonsense to divide up individual names in this way, class-names *are* divisible into those which apply to no individuals, those which apply to exactly one, and those which apply to several. It makes sense also to say that some classes 'exist', either in the sense of having at least one member or in the sense of having exactly one member, and some classes do 'exist' in these senses and some do not. The disappearance of the theorem that there is a non-null class still requires explanation, and so does the type-homogeneity of the arguments of the functor 'ε', but we shall consider these points shortly. Before getting on to that, I want to mention one feature of Leśniew-ski's so-called 'names' which exponents of his theories don't generally make much of, but which seems to me to tell quite conclusively in favour of interpreting them as class-names, namely that they can be *logically complex*. Given any pair of Leśniewskian names we can for instance form their logical product and their logical sum, and we can construct a name which is *logically* empty, e.g. the compound name '*a* and not-*a*'. Russellian variables of lowest type, on the other hand, are logically structureless—you can construct other things out of them, together of course with other symbols; for example, you can construct a one-place predicate (e.g. '— shaves Peter') out of a two-place predicate and a name; but there is nothing out of which you can construct Russellian individual names. (Definite descriptions, e.g. 'the *x* such that *x* shaves Peter' are notoriously *not* 'names' in Russell's view.)

The formal development of a Russellian class theory without variables of the lowest type presents, however, some very taxing problems. For as Russell presents this theory, individual variables are not just an optional appendage which can be lopped off without damaging the rest of the system. On the contrary, Russell regards classes as *logical constructions* out of individuals and functions of individuals. He has so to speak a primary language and a secondary one. In the primary language there are just individual names, functors forming sentences out of these, functors of higher type operating on the preceding functors, and so on. His class theory is merely a set of convenient alternative locutions by which talk about individuals can sometimes be replaced. The basic sentences of this class language are of the form '*x* ε α', asserting an individual's membership of a class, and where 'α' is, say, the class of things that *f*, the form '*x* ε α', '*x* is an *f*-er', is simply a re-writing of '*x f*'s', or more accurately of 'For some $g$, such that if anything $f$'s it $g$'s and vice versa, $x\,g$'s'. And when we wish to define complex classes, for example the logical product of two classes, or the null class, we fall back again and again on this basic form—the logical product of the $\alpha$'s and the $\beta$'s, for example, is the class of $x$'s such that $x$ is an $\alpha$ and $x$ is a $\beta$— these $x$'s, these individual names, are just *not* dispensable.

Leśniewski meets this difficulty by introducing an undefined constant expressing a relation between classes—it can be, but it does not need to be, the functor '$\varepsilon$' previously mentioned. This functor, as I have also previously said, has arguments of the same logical type, so that what it expresses is *not* Russellian class-membership. It expresses rather the *inclusion* of a unit class in another class. This interpretation of the Leśniewskian '$\varepsilon$' was suggested some time ago by Jerzy Łoś, and although Leśniewski himself did not like it, no other interpretation of the symbol seems to me intelligible. It is tantamount to reading the form '$a\ \varepsilon\ b$' as 'The $a$ is a $b$', or 'There is exactly one $a$ and every $a$ is a $b$'. There are of course Russellian forms, though *not* the form '$x\ \varepsilon\ \alpha$', that have this meaning. And the Leśniewskian form '$a = b$' does not express Russellian class identity —'The $a$'s coincide with the $b$'s'—but means rather 'The $a$ is the $b$', that is, 'There is exactly one $a$ and exactly one $b$ and they are the same'. But this is not quite Russellian individual identity either— 'The $a$ is the $a$' is false if there are no $a$'s, or if there are several; but the Russellian '$x = x$' is a law of the system, and is in fact definable as the obvious truism 'For any $f$, if $x\,f$'s then $x\,f$'s'. So if we define individual existence as *Leśniewskian* self-identity, it amounts to a class's being a unit one, and is predicable of some classes but not of others, whereas if we define it as a Russellian self-identity it is predicable of everything a Russellian name can stand for.

Complex classes can also be defined by using the Leśniewskian '$\varepsilon$'. Leśniewski's rules of definition are in fact a little complicated, more complicated than those which are required in Russell's *primary* language, the language of individual names and functors operating on these; but they constitute an interesting solution of a genuine and interesting problem, and they are much tidier than the rules for translating Russell's secondary language, in which he talks about classes, into his primary one; they do not give rise, for example, to scope ambiguities. And while Leśniewski's procedure requires the introduction of a primitive constant that Russell's doesn't need, since Russell can get all the constants he wants in his primary language out of propositional calculus and quantification theory, this very fact gives Leśniewski greater freedom over what his class theory will or will not contain. For this constant '$\varepsilon$', in terms of which existence and non-existence, for example, are definable, must have special axioms laid down for it, and it is easy enough so to choose these axioms that the formula 'For some *a*, the *a* exists', or 'For some *a*, the *a* is the *a*' is not a theorem. No Leśniewskian denies that it is a truth, but it is not a provable truth in Leśniewski's system. From Russell's system, on the other hand, it is impossible to delete this theorem, for what Russell means by the non-emptiness of the universe is that for some *x*, *x* is *x*, that is, for some *x*, for every *f*, if *x f*'s then *x f*'s, and this is provable from propositional calculus and quantification theory alone. Or if we *can* eliminate it by attaching complicated provisos to the ordinary rules of quantification, the resulting system is very difficult to interpret.

It is profitable at this stage to ask ourselves whether the appearance of this theorem in *Principia Mathematica* really does indicate a 'defect in logical purity', and if so what is the source of this infection. Basically it comes from the interpretation of Russell's lowest-type variables as standing for *individual names*, that is to say symbols whose only contribution to what is actually said by the sentences in which they occur is the identification of the individual objects that the sentences are about. If *such* a symbol fails to identify any individual object, the sense of the sentence is incomplete and nothing is really said. Using the word 'This' as a symbol of this sort, what is said by 'This exists' is bound to be either a truth or nothing at all. Hence the assumption that there are complete statements of the form '*fx*', where '*x*' is a symbol of this kind, already involves the non-emptiness of the universe. One way of purging logic of this assumption would be to conceive quantification theory as being concerned simply with the application of quantifiers to functors with their arguments, without regard to what parts of speech these functors and arguments are. The *form* of quantification theory would in fact be unchanged if we interpreted Russell's lowest-type variables as standing for *Leśniewskian* 'names', that is to say class names, and his predicates for functors forming sentences out of these. The form 'For some *x*, for all *f*, if *fx* then *fx*', or as we might now prefer to write it 'For some *a*, for all *f*, if *fa* then *fa*' would still be provable from propositional calculus and quantification theory alone, and indeed it is so provable in ontology, but it now carries no existential implications, since an *a* that would instantiate it could be an empty class.

If, however, we may regard Russell's interpretation of his lowest-type variables as an extra-logical matter, we may equally so regard the undefined constant which is required in ontology. For as we have seen we can define existence in terms of this constant, and we can *formulate* the proposition that for some *a*, the *a* exists, even if we so choose our axioms that we cannot prove it. Such a choice of axioms seems, indeed, strangely arbitrary—the proposition concerned is, after all, formulated purely in terms of the constants and variables of the system, and is acknowledged to be true, so *if* those constants are regarded as purely logical, why is the truth not so regarded? I cannot really see much sense in this.

It may seem from what I have said that ontology, on my interpretation of it, is committed to the existence of classes as nameable entities, though in fact Leśniewski was notoriously nominalistic. But this is a misunderstanding, arising from the use of the perhaps unfortunate term 'class-name'. What we have to do with here are *common nouns*, and these are not strictly speaking *names of objects* at all. When we read the Russellian '$x \, \varepsilon \, \alpha$' as '$x$ is a member of the class of $\alpha$'s', for example, 'Russell is a member of the class of men', this looks as if we are asserting a relation between a concrete object and an abstract one, but the theory of types itself should warn us that this is not quite right, and we might do better to read the form simply as '$x$ is an $\alpha$', for example 'Russell is a man'. Here the form 'is a' is not quite a proper verb, that is a functor which makes sentences out of individual names; rather it makes a sentence out of a name and a common noun. And the functors which join the $a$'s and $b$'s in ontology, and the $\alpha$'s and $\beta$'s in class theory, are not, properly speaking, predicates; they are functors like 'Every — is a —', 'The — is a —', 'There is no such thing as a —'. In fact, these functors which take arguments of Leśniewski's lowest type include ordinary numerical functors, like 'There is exactly one —', 'There are exactly forty-three —s', and so on. It is no doubt convenient to use forms like 'The class of $a$'s is an empty class', 'The class of $a$'s is a member of the class of pairs', and so on, and Leśniewski introduces a higher-order '$\varepsilon$' which is so defined that '$f \, \varepsilon \, g$' may be read as 'The unit class-of-classes $f$ is included in the class-of-classes $g$'. But these are no more than convenient locutions; 'The class of $a$'s is an empty class', for example, means no more and no less than 'There is no such thing as an $a$', from which the suggestion of naming an abstract object, the class of $a$'s, has been removed.

It is true that Leśniewski quantifies variables of his lowest type, and indeed variables of all types, and there is a doctrine current among some American logicians that any variable subject to quantification thereby counts as standing for a name, but this seems to me a quite eccentric criterion of namehood.

What ontology in fact does is to combine the maxim that only individuals are real with the view that the only way we can linguistically *get at* individuals is by speaking of them as what certain *common* nouns apply to—maybe uniquely; and *that* their application is unique is of course something that can be said within the system, *not* by having Russellian individual names in it, but by having as it were an individuating functor, namely the Leśniewskian 'ε' or 'The — is a —'. The phrase 'The so-and-so' is not, as it is in Frege, itself an individual name; there are *no* individual names; but the phrase does occur as part of the larger functor, and so to speak individuates, or purports to individuate, as it makes the full statement. There are many contemporary philosophers, in Oxford for example, who are not very happy about Russellian individual names, and would rather like to do without them, and ontology seems to me worth offering to these philosophers as a system in which their programme is really carried out. In fact it may be far less important as an answer to one of Russell's prayers than as an answer to one of the prayers of the *anti*-Russellians. Leśniewski's own system is, indeed, characterized by an extreme extensionalism which is not likely to appeal very much to the philosophers I have in mind, and for that matter it doesn't appeal to me either; this extensionalism, moreover, is as thoroughly wrought into Leśniewski's methodology—underlying, for example, his rules of definition—as the use of individual names is wrought into Russell's theory of classes. However, I am sure that with a little trouble one can disentangle the more desirable features of ontology from this less desirable one, just as ontology itself disentangles the pure theory of common nouns from its Russellian name-and-predicate basis.[1]

The difficulty here is perhaps worth illustrating by an example which I have used elsewhere. In ontology one might propose 'defining' the complex term 'thing thought to have wings' in terms of the simpler term 'thing that has wings' and the functor 'it is thought that' by laying down the following equivalence:

> The *a* is a thing thought to have wings if and only if *a* exists and it is thought that the *a* is a thing that has wings.

the proviso ('the *a* exists') on the right-hand side taking care of the point that 'The *a* is a thing thought to have wings' can only be true if there is such a thing as the *a*, though 'It is thought that the *a* is a thing that has wings' only implies that *it is thought that* there is such a thing as the *a*. But even if, let us say, Walter's horse really exists, and someone really does think that Walter's horse is a thing that has wings, it is clear that Walter's horse itself need not be thought to have wings by anyone—show it even to the man who 'thinks that Walter's horse is a thing that has wings', and even he (not knowing or believing that it is Walter's horse) may admit that *that* horse has no wings. Given the Russellian apparatus, the distinction can be made easily enough—the left-hand side of the above equivalence amounts to 'For some *x*, *x* alone is Walter's horse, and it is thought

[1] [Here ends the insertion noted on p. 161.]

that *x* has wings', while the right-hand side amounts to, 'For some *x*, *x* alone is Walter's horse, and it is thought that (for some *x*, *x* alone is Walter's horse and *x* has wings)', where *x* is an individual name variable; and where *x* is an actual individual name, '*x* is thought to have wings' and 'It is thought that *x* has wings' are identical in force, and no proviso about *x*'s existence is needed, since both say nothing at all unless there is something that *x* names. Without Russellian individual names it seems to me that there is no plausible definition of the name-forming functor 'thing thought to be a —' in terms of the sentence-forming functor 'it is thought that —'; the introduction of such functors therefore seems bound to complicate ontology. However, philosophers who are not extensionalists, and who believe that there are not and cannot be any such expressions as Russellian individual names, may well find the complications worth accepting.

While the Leśniewskian and the Russellian theories of names are the ones which so far have been most systematically worked out, I do not wish to deny that there are other possibilities, and in particular it is not impossible to develop a logic for a kind of name that may be either singular or empty, but not plural. One might mention here three recent essays in this direction. In the first place, my Manchester colleague Dr. Lejewski has been developing a logic of 'non-plural names' along Leśniewskian rather than Russellian lines. Such names are capable of logical complexity, and their logic requires a special functor with its own special axiom or axioms. This functor could be, for example, Leśniewskian individual identity, the form '*a* = *a*' being true when the name '*a*' applies to one object and false when it applies to none. The problems involved here are perhaps partly analogous to those arising with 'Aristotelian' names, i.e. ones which may be singular or plural but not empty. When complex names are introduced into a system of this sort, one needs to guard against allowing modes of composition which could result in some of the compound names being empty, e.g. even if both the names '*a*' and '*b*' have application, it does not follow that the conjunctive name '*a*-and-*b*' will do so (there may be things that are *a*'s and things that are *b*'s, but nothing that is at once an *a* and a *b*). Analogously, if a name, say 'Socrates', is non-plural, it does not follow that, e.g., 'non-Socrates' will be so—there would seem to be millions of non-Socrateses. Lejewski solves this problem by employing a 'definition-frame' which only permits the introduction of names like 'he that is uniquely not Socrates', which works out as empty if there are many who are not Socrates; though the *verb* 'is-not-Socrates', which can also be defined in Lejewski's system, may apply to many objects.

---

[1] *Proceedings of the Aristotelian Society*, Suppl. 38 (1963), 127–46.

A rather different theory of non-plural names is adumbrated by Dr. A. Kenny in his contribution to a recent symposium on 'Oratio Obliqua'.[1] 'Names', in Kenny's sense, as in Russell's, are logically structureless, and N is a name if, and only if, its user intends to refer to a single object, say B, by it. If this object B exists, N is a name *of* B, and *refers* to B, and sentences containing N are *about* B; but if there is no such object, all we can say is that the user *means* B by it, and that his sentences *mention* B. Names, even when empty, are not in general mere abridgements of Russellian definite descriptions, though any user of a name must have in mind some definite description which he would apply to the object he means by it, and the expression 'B' *will* abridge this definite description in any sentences of the form 'B exists' or 'B does not exist'.

My own principal problem about 'names' in this sense is that I cannot extract from Kenny's paper any clear account of how they are used in reported speech.[1] Let us see how Kenny applies his theory to statements like 'Paul thinks that Elmer is a fellow traveller'. He says that Paul, if he expresses this uncharitable thought of his, will use the word 'Elmer' as a name, and will mean Elmer by it, but the person who uses the whole utterance, i.e. 'Paul thinks that Elmer is a fellow traveller', will not, in general, be using the word 'Elmer' as a name, and could make this utterance in its usual sense even if he knew that there was no such person as Elmer. My question here is just this: if the reporter *isn't* in this case using 'Elmer' as a name, how *is* he using it? Is he using it as a disguised definite description? According to Kenny, he *would* be using it as a disguised definite description if he actually said 'There is no such person as Elmer'. But what if he knows that there is no such person as Elmer, but simply *says*, 'Paul thinks that Elmer is a fellow traveller'? Is he *then* using 'Elmer' as a disguised definite description? If he is not, Kenny doesn't tell us what else he *is* doing, and if he *is*, it would seem that he is not, on Kenny's account, giving an accurate report of what Paul thinks; for what his report means, if he is using 'Elmer' as a definite description, is that Paul thinks that the so-and-so (whatever it is) is a fellow traveller, while what Paul actually thinks, according to Kenny, is not that the so-and-so is a fellow traveller but that *Elmer* is.

Nor is this just a rather recondite matter which we can safely ignore; the difficulty affects the whole of Kenny's own metalinguistic remarks themselves. It affects, for example, the sentence that I used

[1] [In the MS. of 'Names' the argument against Kenny is stated very succinctly; for this appendix we have replaced it with the fuller statement which Prior wrote for oral delivery at the Joint Session of the Mind Association and Aristotelian Society of 1963.]

a minute ago when trying to think myself into Kenny's position—the sentence 'What Paul thinks is not that the so-and-so is a fellow traveller but that Elmer is'. How am *I*, in the person of Kenny, supposed to be using the word 'Elmer' here? If as a definite description, then I fail to make the distinction I am trying to make; yet I cannot be using it as a name, that is I cannot be intending to refer to Elmer by it, because *ex hypothesi* I know perfectly well that I cannot possibly refer to Elmer by it, since there is no such person.

Paul, on Kenny's view, *means Elmer* by the word 'Elmer', but what does Kenny mean by it when he *says* that Paul means Elmer by it? Does *he* mean Elmer by it? But to mean Elmer is to intend to refer to Elmer, and *ex hypothesi* Kenny cannot intend this. And if, on the other hand, he is here using 'Elmer' as a definite description, he is telling us that Paul means the so-and-so by it. Here we either understand the phrase 'the so-and-so' as having quotes around it or we don't. If we don't, when we say that Paul means the so-and-so, we mean that there is a unique so-and-so to which Paul thus relates himself; but *ex hypothesi* there isn't, and we know there isn't. If we *do* intend quotes round the phrase, we are saying that Paul means by the word 'Elmer' what is meant by the phrase 'the so-and-so'; but on Kenny's view Paul *isn't* using the word as a disguised definite description, so that this *isn't* what he means by it.

In short, I don't think this use of the term 'name' will work, in any consistent way. My own view of these matters is the simple one that if Elmer doesn't exist he can no more be meant by a name than he can be kicked by a foot, and this is so regardless of whether this name (or foot, as the case may be) be used by someone who believes in Elmer's existence or by someone who doesn't.

Another theory of non-plural names is developed, rather more systematically on the formal side, in some recent work on modal logic and kindred topics by Hintikka, Kanger, and Kripke.[1] In my own treatment, in *Time and Modality*, of the use of Russellian names in modal and similar contexts, I have assumed that in possible (or imaginary, or past, or future) states of affairs from which the object $x$ is absent there can be no sentences in which $x$ is properly named, and no facts which concern $x$; and modal logic (or belief logic, or tense logic) must be complicated in certain ways in order to allow for this possibility. Kripke, who has perhaps developed most fully the alternatives to this view, has systems in which all *simple* sentences in which $x$ is properly named count as false in all states of affairs in which $x$ is non-existent, and the truth-values of complex sentences follow

[1] See, in particular, the papers of Hintikka and Kripke in the proceedings of the 1962 Helsinki colloquium on Non-classical Logics, *Acta Philosophica Fennica*, 16 (1963), 65–94.

from this decision by various rules (e.g. all negations of simple sentences work out as being, in these circumstances, true). It may be
noted that this view gives a certain absoluteness to the distinction
between simple and complex sentences and facts which is not necessary in my own treatment of the subject.

In Kripke's system, as in Kenny's, names appear to be logically
structureless; but, as in Lejewski's, there is nothing to prevent a
disbeliever in Moloch's existence from using 'Moloch' as a genuine
name—as the name, presumably, of an object in a merely imagined
or possible universe. Kripke's formal development of this point of
view is impeccable, but it seems to me philosophically objectionable
because it makes certain questions seem genuine ones which I am
fairly certain are spurious. For example, suppose a child imagines he
has a friend called 'Jack McKellar' about whom he builds various
fantasies, and another child, or perhaps an adult, teases the first child
by developing the fantasies in directions to which he objects (e.g. by
saying that Jack McKellar is known as 'Black' Jack McKellar to his
friends). A quarrel is then likely to arise as to whether the Jack
McKellars referred to by the two people are the same or different
individuals, and similar questions and disputes may be concocted
about the identity of merely possible and merely future individuals.

The totality of objects in existence at a given *past* time, on the other
hand, has a certain definiteness which makes it less objectionable to
regard them as properly nameable, and I should like to see whether
a Kripke-like account of them could be combined with something
more like my own account of merely future and merely possible ones
without any awkward consequences (such as inconsistency, or the
denial of the continuity of time).

# SELECT BIBLIOGRAPHY

ANSCOMBE, G. E. M., 'The Intentionality of Sensation', in *Analytical Philosophy* (ed. R. J. Butler), 2nd series, Oxford, 1965, pp. 156–80.

AQUINAS, *De Veritate*.

ARISTOTLE, *Metaphysics*.

AUSTIN, J. L., *Philosophical Papers*, Oxford, 1961.

BOLZANO, B., *Paradoxes of the Infinite* (tr. D. A. Steele), London, 1950.

BRENTANO, Franz, *Psychologie vom empirischen Standpunkt*, Leipzig, 1876.

CARROLL, Lewis, *Symbolic Logic*, 4th edn., New York, 1958.

CARTWRIGHT, R., 'Propositions', in *Analytical Philosophy* (ed. R. J. Butler), 1st series, Oxford, 1962, pp. 81–103.

CHISHOLM, R. M., 'The Ethics of Requirement', *American Philosophical Quarterly*, 1 (1964), 1–7.

—— 'Intentionality', in *The Encyclopaedia of Philosophy* (ed. Edwards), New York, 1967.

COHEN, L. J., *The Diversity of Meaning*, London, 1962.

FEYS, R., 'La Technique de la logique', *Revue Philosophique de Louvain* (1946), 74–103, 237–70.

FINDLAY, J. N., *Values and Intentions*, London, 1961.

—— *Meinong's Theory of Objects and Values*, Oxford, 1965.

FREGE, G., *Philosophical Writings* (ed. P. T. Geach and M. Black), Oxford, 1952.

GEACH, P. T., *Reference and Generality*, Ithaca, 1962.

HARRAH, D., 'The Logic of Questions and Answers', *Philosophy of Science*, 28 (1961), 40–6.

HOFSTADTER, A., and McKINSEY, J. C. C., 'On the Logic of Imperatives', *Philosophy of Science*, 6 (1939), 446–57.

JOHNSON, W. E., *Logic*, Cambridge, 1921.

KEYNES, J. N., *Formal Logic*, 4th edn., London, 1906.

LEJEWSKI, C., 'The Problem of Ontological Commitment', *Fragmenty Filozoficzne Seria Trzecia*, Księga Pamiątkowa ku czci Prof. Dr. Tadeusza Kotarbińskiego w Osiemdziesiąta Rocznice Urodzin.

MACKIE, J. L., 'Self-refutation: a Formal Analysis', *Philosophical Quarterly*, 14 (1964), 2–12.

MAKINSON, D. K., 'The Paradox of the Preface', *Analysis*, 25 (1964–5), 205–7.

MILL, J. S., *System of Logic*, London, 1843.

MOORE, G. E., *Some Main Problems of Philosophy*, London, 1953.

—— *Commonplace Book 1919–1953* (ed. C. Lewy), London, 1963.

PEIRCE, C. S., *Collected Papers* (ed. C. Hartshorne, P. Weiss, and A. W. Burks), Harvard, 1958.

PRICE, H. H., *Hume's Theory of the External World*, Oxford, 1940.

PRIOR, A. N., 'Entities', *Australasian Journal of Philosophy*, 32 (1954), 159–68.

—— 'Berkeley in Logical Form', *Theoria*, 21 (1955), 117–22.

PRIOR, A. N., 'Definitions, Rules and Axioms', *Proceedings of the Aristotelian Society*, 56 (1955–6), 199–216.

—— 'On a Family of Paradoxes', *Notre Dame Journal of Formal Logic*, 2 (1961), 16–32.

—— 'Indirect Speech Again', *Philosophical Studies*, 14 (1963), 12–15.

—— 'Is the Concept of Referential Opacity really Necessary?', *Acta Philosophica Fennica*, 16 (1963), 189–200.

—— 'Oratio Obliqua', *Proceedings of the Aristotelian Society*, Suppl. 37 (1963), 115–26.

—— 'Indirect Speech and Extensionality', *Philosophical Studies*, 15 (1964), 35–8.

—— 'The Done Thing', *Mind*, 73 (1964), 441–2.

—— 'Correspondence Theory of Truth', in *The Encyclopaedia of Philosophy* (ed. Edwards), New York, 1967.

QUINE, W. V., *Word and Object*, M.I.T., 1960.

—— *From a Logical Point of View*, Harvard, 1961.

RAMSEY, F. P., *Foundations of Mathematics*, London, 1931.

REID, T., *Essays on the Intellectual Powers of Man*, M.I.T., 1969.

RUSSELL, B. A. W., *Principia Mathematica*, Cambridge, 1910–13.

—— *Introduction to Mathematical Philosophy*, London, 1919.

—— *Problems of Philosophy*, London, 1912.

—— *The Analysis of Mind*, London, 1921.

—— 'The Philosophy of Logical Atomism', in *Logic and Knowledge* (ed. R. C. Marsh), London, 1956, pp. 175–281.

RYLE, G., 'Are There Propositions?', *Proceedings of the Aristotelian Society*, 30 (1929–30), 91–126.

SHORTER, J. M., 'Facts, Logical Atomism and Reducibility', *Australasian Journal of Philosophy*, 40 (1962), 283–302.

STRAWSON, P. F., 'Truth', *Proceedings of the Aristotelian Society*, Suppl. 24 (1950), 134–7.

TARSKI, A., 'The Concept of Truth in Formalized Language', in *Logic, Semantics, Metamathematics*, Oxford, 1956, pp. 152–278.

WILSON, J. C., *Statement and Inference*, Oxford, 1926.

WISDOM, J., 'Logical Constructions', *Mind*, 40–2 (1931–3).

WITTGENSTEIN, L., *Tractatus Logico-Philosophicus*, London, 1922.

—— *Philosophical Investigations*, Oxford, 1953.

# INDEX

Compiled by Mary Prior

PRINTED IN GREAT BRITAIN
AT THE UNIVERSITY PRESS, OXFORD
BY VIVIAN RIDLER
PRINTER TO THE UNIVERSITY